A–Z GUIDE TO
CLEANING, CONSERVING
AND REPAIRING ANTIQUES

Tom Rowland

revised by
Noël Riley

Constable · London

First published in Great Britain 1981
by Constable and Company Ltd
3 The Lanchesters, 162 Fulham Palace Road
London W6 9ER
Revised edition 1995
Copyright © 1981, 1995 by the Estate of Tom Rowland
The right of Tom Rowland to be
identified as the author of this work
has been asserted in accordance
with the Copyright, Designs and Patents Act 1988
ISBN 0 09 474250 2
Set in Linotron Sabon by
Rowland Phototypesetting Ltd
Bury St Edmunds, Suffolk
Printed in Great Britain by
St Edmundsbury Press Ltd
Bury St Edmunds, Suffolk

A CIP catalogue record for this book
is available from the British Library

Contents

Acknowledgements 7

How to use this book 9

Introduction 11

Section One: Items to be Cleaned and Repaired 15

Section Two: Materials, Equipment and Techniques 147

Section Three: Directory of Suppliers and Organizations 173

Further reading 187

Index 188

Acknowledgements

In preparing this edition I have been helped by many people who have given their time and knowledge most generously. I would especially like to thank Pam and Jack Adams, Wendy Allen (Goslings, Sudbury), Lucy Askew, Catherine Barker, Stephanie Burns (Boots, Sudbury), Theresa Courtauld, Cresswell Hardware (Sudbury), Joanne Dixey, Christopher Dobson, Trevor Farthing (Acton Square Building Supplies, Sudbury), Paul Goodman (National Museum of Photography, Film and Television), Keith Harding, Martin Hinchcliffe (National Army Museum), Peter Hornsby, Stephen Jarrett (Witney Antiques), Paul Jago (Recollect Studios), Julia Korner, John Lawson (Picreator Enterprises), Nick McKenzie, Michal Morse (The Dolls' House), Ken Newson (The Clock and Barometer Studio, Sudbury), Adrian Smith (West Dean College), Roy Thomson (Leather Conservation Centre), Lucilla Watson, and my husband, Peter Owen.

My greatest debt of gratitude must be to the late Tom Rowland, who wrote the first edition of this A–Z guide and whose arrangement we have followed in the present one.

Noël Riley

How to use this book

This book is arranged in alphabetical order in three sections.

Section One gives directions for the care of the most common categories of COLLECTABLE ANTIQUES. It deals with cleaning and conservation, and simple techniques of renovation and repair.

Section Two lists the **materials** recommended for cleaning and repairing, with details of their specialized uses and sources of supply.

Section Three gives addresses of specialized suppliers and useful organisations, and references to this are indicated by an * in Sections One and Two.

Cross-references to Section One are indicated by CAPITALS, and to Section Two by **bold type**.

While we have taken care only to recommend conservative procedures, the Publishers cannot be held responsible for any damage resulting from their pursuit.

How to Use This Book

Introduction

Since the first edition of this book was published nearly fifteen years ago, there have been fundamental changes in caring for antiques as well as in the products and equipment available to the carers. The general view among conservators that less is more and that all procedures should be reversible has percolated from museum conservation departments through to collectors of the humblest artefacts. On the whole we are much more wary of the damage we can do by over-enthusiastic tampering and we are beginning to learn, often the hard way, what professional conservators and restorers have been telling us for years: that more damage is done by improper repairs or cleaning than by neglect or natural deterioration, and that such damage is most costly to remedy.

The very notion of renovating antiques has become outdated, replaced by the conservator's ideal of stabilizing past deterioration and protecting from future degradation. The emphasis is on providing conditions which minimize damage and therefore the need for restoration, particularly with regard to levels of light, temperature and humidity. When intervention is necessary, it should be with the least invasive method that will work.

We should respect our antiques for what they are – old – and not expect them to look new. This may mean learning to live with the odd blemish and accepting that dents, scratches, stains or cracks are part of an object's history and need not detract from its interest, beauty or usefulness. Equally it may involve difficult decisions with regard to reversing old repairs or changing 'incorrect' replacement parts. Knowing what *not* to do is as important as knowing how to do it. It is all too easy to go too far.

Another change has been the expansion of the conservation and restoration industries, which are themselves more connected with each other than once they were. There are more and better qualified specialists to consult in practically every field of art and antiques than there were fifteen years ago: high calibre expertise has become accessible to ordinary collectors.

At the same time the products available to both professional and amateur carers and repairers have multiplied. Many have been developed by and for conservators and are safe and reliable to use, while some are based on well-tried traditional recipes or techniques. It is worth noting here that human spit is one of the most effective cleaning substances as well as the cheapest: old-fashioned 'spit and polish' has few equals in the everyday care of antiques. While products offering instant cure-alls or magic remedies should be regarded with caution, many of them are useful, if used with discrimination and care.

Nearly all the suppliers listed at the back of the book provide catalogues of their products and many will give excellent practical advice. Some issue book lists or sell specialist technical manuals. Staff in art and craft shops are usually knowledgeable about the products they sell: do not be shy to ask them questions. For specialist information, consult the list of organizations.

Users of the first edition of the *A–Z Guide* may be disappointed to find that some of the original recipes have been omitted, while most of the more intrepid procedures recommended then have been replaced with somewhat gentler techniques, which may seem tame in comparison. The book is sprinkled with caveats to leave things alone or to consult an expert in cases of doubt or uncertainty about the wisdom of DIY cleaning or repair, but while it is important to emphasize the risks of careless or irreversible techniques, we have tried to give guidance for cleaning and repairs which can be carried out by the reasonably dextrous amateur without inflicting more damage.

It is unrealistic to expect the average collector or dealer to take every problem to a professional conservator or restorer, and there is much pleasure to be derived from giving an object a face-lift by judicious cleaning, or a new lease of life by a careful repair.

In using this book, certain principles should be observed:

1. Reversible techniques should be used whenever possible: in other words, whatever you do should be done in such a way that it can be undone at a future date without further damage to the object.
2. Conservation, cleaning or repairs should never add to deterioration.
3. Objects made of several materials should be looked after in conditions to suit the most vulnerable.
4. Mention of acid-free conditions implies an awareness that woods like oak and chestnut and materials like velvet, wool and felt are all acid-producing, as well as the knowledge that card, paper or tissue used in display or storage should be acid-free.
5. Unless otherwise specified, references in this book to 'soapy water' mean lukewarm water with non-ionic detergent (Synperonic N). This is virtually free of additives or surfactants and is the safest soap-and-water solution to use with delicate materials. It is also one of the least effective, so expect modest rather than dazzling results.
6. Always use best quality cotton wool where this is mentioned; impurities and lumps can be damaging.

7. Brushes should be real hair or bristle, and not nylon, and the softest that will do the job in hand should be used. Wash them in warm soapy water (normal household products will do), if necessary removing wax with white spirit first. Use separate brushes, polishing cloths or waddings for different metals.

8. Ensure that all products are clearly labelled and dated: some lose their effectiveness in time. Make sure the tops of containers are always replaced immediately after use.

9. Be rigorous in following the manufacturer's instructions in using materials and equipment, especially if these involve dangerous substances. Always wear protective gloves, mask or goggles if these are indicated, and be careful how you dispose of toxic or flammable wastes – they should never be put down the drain. Contact your local authority for advice on disposal.

Section One
Items to be Cleaned and Repaired

ALABASTER

A form of compressed gypsum, alabaster is usually creamy white or pink with a slight translucency, and veining like marble. However, it is much softer than marble and can easily be chipped or bruised; above all, it is dissolved by water. Alabaster sculptures are therefore not suitable for outdoors. From the thirteenth century onwards many were designed for church interiors, usually taking the form of painted monuments, but alabaster was used in ancient Egypt, Crete and Greece for statues and portrait plaques, and more recently for clock cases, lamps and vases; it is still carved into ornaments and souvenirs in Near Eastern and Mediterranean countries.

Alabaster should never be cleaned with water. Surface dust can be removed with a soft hair brush or (carefully) with a vacuum cleaner fitted with a fine nozzle. If more rigorous cleaning is called for, use a mixture of half a pint of white spirit, half a pint of distilled water and one teaspoonful of Synperonic N to dampen cotton wool swabs. Wipe the piece from the bottom upwards, discarding the swabs as they become dirty. Rinse with swabs dampened with white spirit only and dry with white kitchen paper or a clean tea towel. If stains persist, use Bell 1967 Cleaner. Polishing with a **microcrystalline wax** can restore and protect the surface.

Repairs to breaks in alabaster should be made with reversible **adhesives** such as HMG, Bostik or UHU All Purpose clear adhesive, while missing chips and other small areas can be filled with an epoxy resin **filler** such as Milliput or Sylmasta.

ALUMINIUM

This silvery, malleable material was known as a precious curiosity as far back as the time of Elizabeth I: her treasury included an aluminium teaspoon 'valued above all else'. It re-emerged at the Paris Exhibition of 1855, and by 1886 new techniques had reduced manufacturing costs. Since the end of the nineteenth century it has been used for decorative items, the most famous example being Alfred Gilbert's cast aluminium sculpture of Eros in Piccadilly, London.

Aluminium is attacked by caustic preparations, and can be corroded by contact with other metals, so take care not to expose it to them. The surface of twentieth-century pieces has frequently been dyed in a variety of colours by the process of anodizing. Because it is such a soft metal, the use of any but the mildest **abrasives** will cause damage. If the surface shows the hard white deposits symptomatic of corrosion through oxidization, wipe it with a damp cloth, or with cotton wool swabs moistened with methylated spirit. If stains persist, try a very mild abrasive such as jeweller's rouge, Prelim or Solvol Autosol. Once the aluminium surface has been cleaned, use **microcrystalline wax polish** to protect and enhance its appearance.

AMBER

Amber is the fossilized resin from an extinct variety of pine tree. There are two different varieties: the more common is honey-coloured, while the other is darker brown, rather like tortoiseshell. Lumps of amber sometimes contain petrified flower and insect parts, and even small whole flies; these are much sought after. It is easy to carve and polish and is often

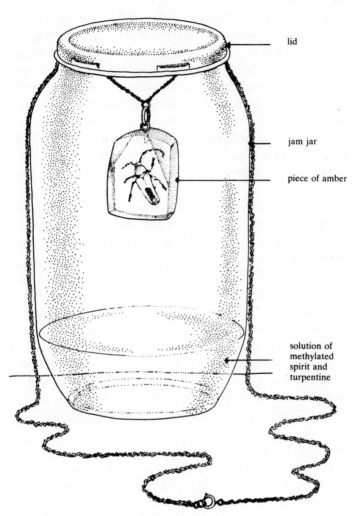

lid

jam jar

piece of amber

solution of
methylated
spirit and
turpentine

suspended with twine, thread or chain

How to clean a piece of amber

17

used in jewellery and *objets d'art*; its lustre improves with wear and handling. If rubbed with a woollen cloth, amber generates static electricity and attracts fluff, scraps of paper and dust, much as a magnet attracts iron filings. Rubbing also releases a pleasant smell of pine forests, with a hint of musk.

The smell is important as it is one of the ways of differentiating amber from imitations, which can be very realistic, right down to the embedded flies and flower seeds. A drop or so of ether on the object can also sometimes indicate a plastic fake: synthetic material will melt and become cloudy on the surface. However, this will not reveal false amber made from glass or ambroid (heated and compressed chips of amber).

Although it is normally translucent, amber may become opaque through exposure to damp, so it should never be washed in water. Nor should it be cleaned with any spirit solvent or alcohol as these will dissolve the surface. Remove dirt by rubbing with french chalk on a soft chamois leather or cotton cloth. Any opacity can usually be removed by keeping the article in a warm, moisture-free atmosphere; but do not overheat. If this treatment is not effective, try suspending the piece above, but not touching, a mixture of one part methylated spirit to three parts artist's turpentine. After treatment, bring up the surface with **microcrystalline wax polish**. Repairs may be made with a reversible **adhesive** such as PVA, HMG, Bostik or UHU All Purpose.

ARMS AND ARMOUR

Practically all guns, edged weapons and armour consist of one or more metals, with or without other materials, and it is the care of the metalwork that is the chief concern in looking after these objects. The conservation of arms and armour is highly specialized, and much damage can be done by the unwary: restoration of rare, valuable or very complicated pieces should be undertaken by a professional conservator. When handling weapons, guns or armour you should wear cotton or surgical gloves: fingermarks on the metalwork are corrosive and can be indelible.

Edged weapons should be removed from their sheaths or scabbards with great care by pointing them downwards and holding the scabbard at the top. If the blade has become rusted into a metal scabbard, you can use penetrating **oil** to free it (but not if the sheath or scabbard is made of leather). After allowing the oil to work, for a day or so if necessary, hold the scabbard secure in a vice, protecting it from the steel jaws with pieces of softwood. Gently tap the hilt, or a piece of wood placed on top of the hilt, in different directions with a rubber or plastic hammer until it is loosened and you can withdraw the blade.

Cleaning the blade requires care, especially if it is engraved or inlaid. Use the finest wire wool soaked in a mixture of light lubricating oil and paraffin. Bad rust may be scraped off piece by piece with a scalpel, or loosened with oil before being rubbed with wire wool. Do not use chemical rust removers. Finish with a protective covering of **microcrystalline wax**. Armour calls for similar treatment.

Handles, hilts and scabbards must obviously be treated according to their material. Many scabbards are leather-covered, and damaged examples can be re-covered without much difficulty. Soak a thin piece of leather of suitable size in water to make it supple; ease it into place over the metal or wood base and sew along the edges with shoemaker's thread (from a shoe repairer). While it is still damp, it may be embossed or tooled into patterns. Finally, colour and polish it with shoe polish.

When guns are in good condition the only maintenance they need is an occasional oiling with a light machine oil such as 3-in-1. Remember that locks, springs and other hidden parts of the mechanism need attention to prevent rust. A humid atmosphere is enough to cause rusting of unprotected iron and steel. Sometimes lacquer is used, but this is not recommended.

When a firearm of any description first comes into your possession, check that it is not loaded. With muzzle loaders, slide a piece of dowel down the barrel, mark its length and measure it against the outside of the barrel. If you find it is charged, you must take the greatest care in removing the ball, wad and powder. If you have a cleaning rod, it is likely to have a fitting which can be screwed into the ball; if not, play safe and take it to a gunsmith.

Check all parts of the gun to make sure they are in good condition; take care when testing the lock mechanism, which can fracture if not handled correctly. In particular the main spring may fracture if you pull the hammer back without looking inside the lock first to check the condition of the spring. If you intend to strip down and clean a gun yourself, make sure you know exactly how to reassemble it: if in doubt, consult a specialist before dismantling.

The general procedure is as follows. First the lock should be removed, usually by unscrewing it from the stock; always put it to half-cock. Screws are likely to be corroded or rusted and care is needed not to tear the slots (see SCREWS for methods of loosening). Next, remove the barrel, butt cap, ramrod well and trigger guard. These are all secured either with screws or pins. For tapping out pins, use a brass or other soft metal rod, taking care not to splinter the wooden part of the gun.

Once the gun is stripped, any rust should be removed with a mixture of paraffin and gun oil (soak the parts overnight) or with a **rust remover** such as Biox or Renaissance De-corroder. For polishing, use fine wire wool and Plus Gas, or Solvol Autosol. This will produce a brilliant shine. You should now give all the metal parts a thin covering of rifle oil or Renaissance wax. If the weapon is to be fired, clean the interior of the barrel with a cleaning rod; if it is pitted or shows other signs of wear, consult a gunsmith before trying it out. Never try to 'fire' a gun by bringing it to full cock and pulling the trigger: hold the hammer and release it slowly.

BAMBOO

The wooden parts of the gun will also require cleaning. Fine steel wool lubricated with white spirit, or methylated spirit mixed (half and half) with water will remove grease and dirt; rub along the grain to avoid scratches. Perished varnish or persistent grime can be removed with a **paint stripper** such as Nitromors, which should be neutralized with white spirit after treatment. Finally, polish butts and stocks with wax **furniture polish**, or with boiled linseed oil.

Dents in wooden parts can be reduced and sometimes removed completely by applying a damp cloth pad or cotton wool to the bruised area. The moisture will cause the fibres of the wood to swell, thus reducing the blemish. This treatment may take two or three days to be effective.

BAIZE

Green or red baize is the usual covering for the inner surfaces of games tables and screens, for protection on the bottoms of boxes such as tea caddies and, in large old houses, for covering doors between the kitchen quarters and reception rooms. Baize should be cleaned by vacuuming. Liquid spills should be soaked up with kitchen paper or a clean linen cloth as soon as possible. Stains may sometimes be mitigated by swabbing with a cloth damped in soapy water, but do not rub too vigorously. Baize is particularly vulnerable to moth; keeping it clean is the best preventative, but vigilance and treatment of the first signs of infestation are obviously important.

To replace damaged baize, follow the directions given for replacing leather on desks and tables (see LEATHER).

BAMBOO

Bamboo furniture has enjoyed waves of popularity since the late eighteenth century. In his *Cabinet Dictionary* (1803), Sheraton defines bamboo as 'a kind of Indian reed, which in the East is used for chairs,' but tables, cabinets, stands and other furniture of bamboo were much used for interiors

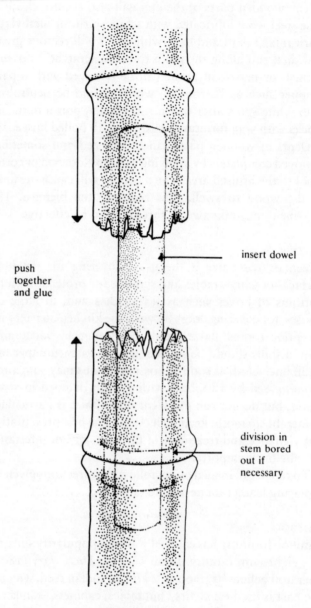

push
together
and glue

insert dowel

division in
stem bored
out if
necessary

Repairing bamboo

decorated in the Chinese taste of the Regency period. A great deal of imitation bamboo furniture, of turned and painted beech, was also made. Bamboo continued to be used for small items of furniture throughout the Victorian period, and these pieces are now much collected.

Clean bamboo by scrubbing it with warm soapy water and a nail brush. Dry carefully and treat with transparent wax polish.

Bamboo, a form of dried grass with a hollow stem, does not break in the same way as wood, but it does splinter. When this happens, support the break by inserting a length of dowel in the hollow centre. If you need to cut the cane, do so at one of the nodules where the break will be all but invisible; if necessary, drill out a hole deep enough for the dowel to extend into the next section of the cane. Using animal glue or PVA, push the splintered sections together and bind in place with masking tape until the adhesive is dry. Later, remove the binding, rub down with fine sandpaper and wax the surface.

BAROMETERS

The first barometer, a column of mercury enclosed in a glass tube with the open end standing in a reservoir open to the atmosphere, was invented by Evangelista Torricelli in 1643. Improvements to this siphon principle were soon being manufactured in other parts of Europe, particularly Britain.

It was further developed into the siphon or wheel barometer, consisting of a U-tube with one arm 30 inches long, closed at the end, and one short arm 3–4 inches long, open to the atmosphere. The mercury-filled tube hangs off a vacuum at its closed end, while a glass weight floats on the mercury at the open end. The glass weight is connected by a silk cord running over a pulley to another, smaller, counterbalance weight. Through its size the pulley amplifies the movement of the mercury and transmits it to a hand which rotates as the level of the mercury rises and falls with the

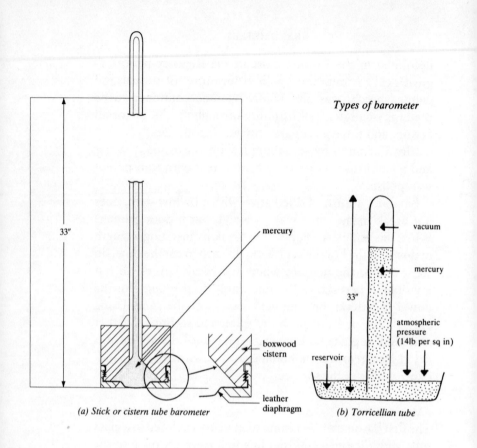

Types of barometer

(a) Stick or cistern tube barometer

mercury

boxwood cistern

leather diaphragm

33″

vacuum

mercury

atmospheric pressure (14lb per sq in)

reservoir

33″

(b) Torricellian tube

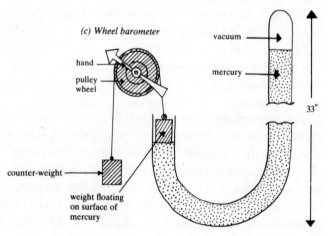

(c) Wheel barometer

hand

pulley wheel

counter-weight

weight floating on surface of mercury

vacuum

mercury

33″

variation in atmospheric pressure, indicating changes in the weather.

The English scientist Robert Hooke (1635–1703) developed the wheel or banjo barometer in Britain, on the same siphon principle. He first put the words 'rain', 'change', 'fair', 'set fair' etc. on a dial. Both stick and wheel barometers were being sold in London from the 1680s onwards; another variant, dating from the eighteenth century, was the diagonal or signpost barometer. Most stick barometers have a reservoir of mercury contained in a leather-bottomed vessel within a wooden cover.

In the aneroid barometer, developed in the nineteenth century, the variation in atmospheric pressure is recorded by a sensitive metal diaphragm covering a circular metal vessel containing a partial vacuum. Slight variations in pressure cause a spring and a gear train to turn the recording pointer.

Great care must be taken in moving or inspecting barometers, especially of the mercury type. They must not be laid flat, but supported at an angle of 45 degrees with the top uppermost. Move them gently: a sudden jerk can cause the mercury to break up, or even to break the glass. If the mercury leaks out for any reason, clear it up at once (but not with a vacuum cleaner) as the vapour is poisonous. Put it into a closed container and do not let it come into contact with silver or gold. Always wash your hands after touching it.

A sticking needle or pointer in a siphon type of barometer may mean that dirt has built up in the tube and contaminated the mercury, which turns into a paste which cannot move freely. It may be possible to have the mercury cleaned and replaced. This procedure, like changing a broken tube, is a job for a professional.

A stick barometer with a leather reservoir is easier to manage: the brass screw at the base can be tightened to raise the column of mercury to the top of the tube, which makes it more secure for transport.

The scales on barometers may be of silvered brass, ivory, bone, parchment, paper, glass or porcelain. Cleaning them will obviously depend on the material, but in considering whether to have a scale plate resilvered, a conservative approach is probably the best one: when in doubt, leave well alone.

Barometers are delicate scientific instruments, and repairs are best left to experts. Correct maintenance will extend their lives and enhance their value. A badly neglected barometer should have a complete overhaul by a reputable specialist.

BASKETWORK

Basketwork is made of woven willow, osier wands or twigs. It should not be confused with RUSHWORK or CANEWORK. Delicate pieces should be dusted with a soft brush or carefully vacuum cleaned. Ingrained dirt can be removed with cotton buds soaked in **non-ionic detergent** and rinsed with clean water; do not soak, and always test coloured pieces for colour fastness before wetting.

More robust items can be cleaned by scrubbing with warm soapy water and then rinsing with a hose. Badly discoloured basketwork can be bleached with diluted hydrogen peroxide.

Old basketwork becomes dry and brittle, and, with loss of flexibility, it breaks easily. It is also vulnerable to woodworm: if necessary, treat with an **insecticide**. Broken basketwork can be glued together with PVA **adhesive**, but on delicate or precious items it is best to secure loose or unravelled fragments by tying them down with neutral-coloured cotton. If whole areas are missing they can be repaired by weaving in suitable twigs of willow or hazel. These are, of course, dry when bought from a handicraft supplier, so soak them well for an hour or so in tepid water.

After cleaning and repairing, leave the article to dry thoroughly and then (for robust items only) polish with wax, using a clean boot brush. If you want to tone down new basket or wickerwork, use a tinted wax polish.

Where basketwork is incorporated into antique furniture and has deteriorated with wear and tear, it is usually best to replace it altogether. Your local association for the blind or the Rural Development Commission* should be able to supply you with the name of a basket weaver.

Lloyd Loom furniture, which is made from machine-made basketwork and is painted, should be cleaned with methylated spirit rather than water, or Vulpex with white spirit.

BEADS

Bead necklaces should not be immersed in water unless they are about to be restrung and are made of wettable materials. If they need cleaning, use a cotton wool bud damped in soapy water and wipe each bead individually. When re-stringing beads, use cotton or silk thread: pearls should

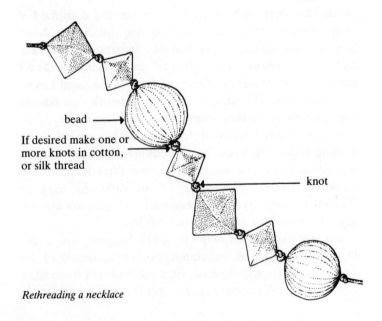

bead

If desired make one or
more knots in cotton,
or silk thread

knot

Rethreading a necklace

always be strung on silk, while coloured beads should be strung on cotton or silk of a blending colour. Use your judgement in deciding whether to tie a knot between each bead.

If the holes through the beads are too small to take even the finest needle, use thin fuse wire to pull the thread through. Alternatively, stiffen the end of the thread with a blob of glue so that it can be threaded through the bead more easily. Attach the clasp by putting the thread through the ring and then back through the end bead before knotting and tying off the thread; push the end of the thread into the hole of the second bead to make a neat finish.

Some beads have sharp edges which can cut through thread and, in consequence, may be better strung on fine wire or chain. Use two pairs of fine flat-nosed pliers to open or close links in necklace chains, and always work sideways to avoid distorting the curves.

BEADWORK

Beads have been embroidered on textiles and costume for many centuries and, strung on to the finest of threads, have been knitted, woven or couched into decorative fabrics for all kinds of purposes. Their great advantage is that beads do not fade like textiles, so their colours remain bright even after centuries. The survival of any beadwork depends on the strength of its base material. If this is very fragile or rotting, you may need to support the piece by sewing it on to a lining of fine nylon net. If the beads are coming away, sew them into place and secure any loose threads. Save any detached beads: replacements of the right size may be difficult to come by. Store beadwork flat, and always use acid-free tissue for wrapping or padding.

It is best to clean beadwork by gentle brushing with a soft brush combined with vacuuming: cover the nozzle of the vacuum cleaner with fine net or a piece of nylon stocking material first. Washing is inadvisable, but, if you do decide this is the best course of action, use lukewarm soapy water and rinse well – never soak the material. Dampness can cause rotting of the underlying threads, so dry the piece carefully with a hairdrier. Do not attempt to wash very precious items, but take them to a textile conservator for cleaning.

BELLOWS

These normally have a wooden front and back, brass nozzle and leather sides. The valve is just a leather flap inside. If this wears out, the bellows have to be opened and the flap replaced. The leather sides may also perish and need renewing.

BLUEJOHN

The translucent fluorspar known as Derbyshire spar or bluejohn (from the French, *bleu-jaune*), with its bold striations of purples, mauves, browns and yellows, was especially popular for decorative objects during the eighteenth century. Much was exported to France, and in England it was used most exotically by Matthew Boulton. Bluejohn vases, candelabra and boxes were usually embellished with ormolu mounts.

Clean it with cotton wool swabs damped in soapy water, taking care not to rub the ormolu mounts. Rinse with swabs damped in clean water and dry; finish with a coat of **microcrystalline wax polish**. Repair with HMG, Bostik or UHU All Purpose clear **adhesive**.

BOOKS

The greatest enemy of books is neglect. Unfortunately it is easy to put them away in a bookcase and forget they are there. Dust, light, damp and central heating can be as harmful as pests like worm, silverfish and book-boring beetle. Temperature and humidity control are very important: too dry an atmosphere results in paper and leather becoming brittle, while damp causes moulds to form on the paper and in the glue of bindings.

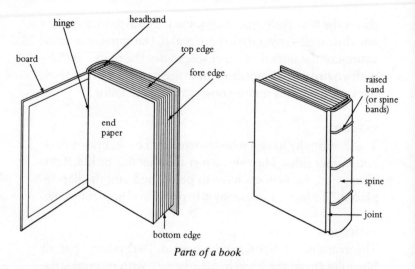

Parts of a book

Books should be dusted regularly, even if they are kept in a closed bookcase. Dust collecting on the tops of the pages will filter down and discolour the top margins. A small hand vacuum cleaner is more effective than a duster and will also help to collect pests lurking within; cover the nozzle with gauze or a piece of nylon stocking. For precious or fragile books, use a soft brush such as an old shaving brush and, holding the book by the fore-edge, dust downwards away from the spine, taking care of the corners and edges of the binding. Never bang books to remove dust. Turned down or cockled pages should be gently straightened out and dusted clean. Remove any paper clips, pins or staples you find.

To remove price tickets from books, first try loosening them by warming with a hairdrier, and then peel very carefully. Residual gum can usually be removed by a dab of white spirit. If you want to remove pencil marks from pages, use a soft eraser and work in straight lines in one direction only, away from the spine. Stop at once if the surface of the paper begins to break down.

Protect damaged or loose books, or those with projecting clasps (which can damage their neighbours), with acid-free card wrappers tied up with tape (not string or elastic).

Leather bindings (but not those of vellum or parchment) can be treated with a dressing such as Connolly's Hide Food or Pliantine. Apply sparingly and allow to dry for twenty-four hours before buffing with a soft cloth. If the surface still feels sticky, wipe with a cloth damped in white spirit. Dry leather spines can sometimes be successfully lubricated by rubbing with a soft neutral soap on a moistened finger. Cloth bindings can be brightened up with Backus book cloth cleaner (from bookbinding suppliers).

Mothballs scattered on the backs of the bookcase shelves will deter most insects, and individual books can be disinfested by placing in an airtight box with mothballs or paradichlorobenzene crystals for a day or so. Better protection can be provided with Mystox (see **Fungicides**). Effective, but less satisfactory, is treatment with Rentokil or Cuprinol low-odour fluids. First remove all the books from the bookcase and then spray the back and shelves. Do not replace books for at least three weeks. Serious infestations may call for Thermo Lignum* treatment.

Mildew will form if the pages of a book have been allowed to become damp. Open the book and stand it on one end with the leaves fanned out. Let them dry in a warmish place, but without direct heat. Once dry, take the book outside, or at least away from other books, and brush the loose mildew deposits off. If it is not obvious, find the cause of the dampness and put it right (see **Fungicides**).

Water damage will result in mould growth if steps are not taken quickly to prevent it. Keep wet books in a cool atmosphere and allow the air to circulate as much as possible, if necessary, by using an electric fan. Flooded books are best kept in the deep freeze (separated while they are in the process of freezing otherwise they will stick together) until they can have the attention of a professional conservator or you have time to deal with them yourself. Take them out one or two at a time and allow them to defrost on clean white blotting paper. Once the book is unfrozen, place blotting paper between the pages and when it becomes damp rather than wet, stand it on end with the leaves fanned out to dry. Freeze drying is better still, especially for precious books: the British Library can advise you on this.

Never use self-adhesive tape on any part of a book. Loose, torn or holed pages can be repaired with Japanese tissue paper or muslin, using starch paste, and protecting surrounding pages with waxed paper (see PAPER). Cracked hinges can also be mended with starch paste or PVA; if the cover has come off a book completely, it should be rebound. If you have a library full of damaged books, you might consider learning the craft of bookbinding.

See also LEATHER.

BOULLE

This ornate tortoiseshell and brass marquetry on furniture and clocks is named after the distinguished French *ébéniste* André-Charles Boulle (1642–1732). The technique was invented much earlier and had been practised in Italy during the sixteenth century, but it was Boulle who developed it and created a new style during the reign of Louis XIV. Brass inlaid furniture, in one form or another, remained fashionable during the eighteenth century but underwent a major revival during the nineteenth, when much Boulle marquetry was reproduced.

The Boulle technique involved gluing together thin sheets of brass and tortoiseshell (often coloured red or green), cutting them into intricate designs and then separating the two materials: the patterns formed could then be fitted into each other to form spectacularly contrasting veneers. Other metals and materials such as mother-of-pearl, bone and horn were also incorporated into some designs.

The brass is likely to become dull with age, and no attempt should be made to bring it back to a bright shine.

Dust it with a brush rather than a duster, to avoid dragging inlays which may have become proud of the surface. Timber surfaces with brass inlays can be polished with furniture wax in the usual way. If a reviver for Boulle marquetry is essential, use a paste made of fine pumice powder mixed with Vaseline and rub it over the surface, taking great care not to lift sections of the veneer. Alternatively, wipe the surface with a damp soapy cloth, rinse, dry thoroughly and then polish with a chamois leather moistened with glycerine.

Because metals do not shrink like wood, brass and other metal inlays in furniture are very prone to springing out and buckling. Repairing such damage may involve cutting and removing parts of the brass inlay in order to hammer them flat, and is best left to specialists. If you do attempt such restorations yourself, clean out all the old glue and dirt from the cavity and make sure the brass section to be reset is a good fit, if necessary by filing it down. Fragments of tortoiseshell can also be reinstated. In either case use animal glue.

If areas of tortoiseshell are missing they can be cosmetically restored using coloured hard wax **fillers** (Liberon). These can be melted like sealing wax, dribbled into the cavity and levelled off when set (see also TORTOISESHELL).

BRASS AND COPPER

The cleaning of dulled brass and copper with household **metal polish** is a simple chore that needs no explanation. What is not generally known is that the interval between cleaning sessions can be considerably extended by polishing the cleaned brass or copper with **microcrystalline wax polish**. The layer of burnished wax forms a skin over the metal which excludes the air and therefore inhibits oxidization.

Metals are more fragile than most people realize, and should be polished as rarely as possible, and with the least abrasive materials that will do the job. For lightly tarnished pieces a wash in mild household detergent followed by a rub with a Long Term Silver Cloth (use a separate one for each different metal) may be enough. Long Term Copper and Brass Cleaner, or impregnated wadding such as Duraglit, should be used for more heavily tarnished items.

When cleaning engraved or embossed surfaces begin by removing old polish and dirt from the crevices with cotton wool buds damped with white spirit; if these accumulations are hard to shift, use a brush dipped in spirit. The metal polish can then be applied and cleaned off with soft brushes (always using separate brushes for each metal).

For cleaning brass fittings such as drawer handles on furniture or finger plates on doors, use a card template to protect the surrounding wood from the metal polish, and finish with a wax polish on the whole surface.

Very heavily tarnished or corroded items can be treated with Prelim, a non-scratch paste, or with a **paint stripper** such as Nitromors, followed by a thorough washing in clean water; then go over it with a metal polish. Abrasive methods, such as metal polish rubbed on with steel wool, should not be necessary. A coat of Ercalene or Joy Transparent Paint can protect brass and copper from tarnishing, but microcrystalline wax polish is usually sufficient.

Small holes can be repaired with epoxy resin **adhesive** mixed to a paste with metallic powder, or with an epoxy **filler** like Kneadable Steel (Bison).

BRITANNIA METAL

This alloy of antimony, copper, lead and tin was used for flatwares and items such as teapots and tankards from the late eighteenth century and was produced in large quantities as a cheap substitute for pewter during the nineteenth century. From the 1840s it was used as a base for electroplating; such pieces are marked EPBM (Electro-Plated Britannia Metal).

Britannia metal is lighter but harder than pewter and is

more brittle than nickel silver or copper which are also used for silver-plating. It tends to fracture rather than dent if roughly handled.

Cleaning should be minimal: like pewter, Britannia metal should have a dark sheen rather than a bright shine on its surface, and an occasional wash in soapy water should be enough. A mild **abrasive** such as Prelim or jeweller's rouge or talc, mixed with a little 3-in-1 oil, can be used to clean off any stains or slight corrosion. Britannia metal which has been electroplated will be easily damaged by abrasives, however; it should be cleaned with Silver Dip or a Long Term Silver Cloth. Lacquering with Frigilene or Joy Transparent Paint may be the best way to protect the surface.

BRONZE

An alloy of copper and tin in varying proportions for different purposes, and sometimes including zinc, tin or lead, bronze is one of the oldest metals known to man; objects made of it are recorded as early as 2000 BC.

When examining or buying bronzes you have to make certain that they are in fact bronze. From Victorian times a large number of statues and figures were cast in spelter (zinc) and then bronzed to look like the genuine article (see ZINC AND SPELTER). More recently, good copies of bronzes have been cast in epoxy resin with bronze powder filling, and these can also be deceptive. Spelter figures are easy to detect by nicking them with a penknife in an unobtrusive place: the bright silvery metal will show through the bronze skin. The cold-cast resin 'bronzes' have a less cold feel and will sound dull if they are tapped.

Bronzes should be cleaned by light dusting, never with metal polish, abrasives, methylated spirit or water, all of which can damage the surface patination or colouring. A gentle brushing with **microcrystalline wax polish**, used sparingly, can restore a dull surface, but take care not to rub off the coloured patina.

Bronzes are particularly damaged by salts: in its most extreme form this damage may result in 'bronze disease', a type of corrosion causing green powdery spots and pitting on the surface. Small areas can be remedied by waxing, but if the disease spreads or is very severe, a specialist conservator should be consulted.

CAMEOS

A cameo is produced when a shell or stone is carved to exploit the different layers of colour within it. The most usual is the shell, carved to form a raised portrait or figurative scene in creamy white on a pink or red background. Various semi-precious stones such as agate, onyx and rock crystal have also been carved into cameos since ancient times, and in the eighteenth century ceramic examples were produced most successfully in Wedgwood's blue jasper ware; coloured glass and pastes have also been used. Nowadays, cameos of plastic may be convincing enough to deceive the unwary collector.

Cameos should not be confused with intaglios, where the design is cut into the stone, as in a seal, rather than appearing as a raised relief carving.

Both cameos and intaglios can be cleaned with warm soapy water, if necessary using a soft brush to get into crevices. If this is not sufficient, try an artist's brush dipped in white spirit, and then wash the piece. Jewellery cleaning dip (Goddard's Jewellery Care) is a good alternative which will also help to brighten up dulled settings.

Broken or chipped cameos can be repaired with an epoxy resin **adhesive** (Araldite), but valuable items should always be taken to a jeweller for repair or resetting.

CAMERAS

Antique cameras are eminently collectable but are not much used for taking photographs. Magic lanterns, on the other hand, are often used for entertainment as they provide the

most convenient means of projecting old lantern slides.
The cleaning of photographic equipment of this kind is
largely common sense. Cameras are a combination of the
crafts of the instrument maker, cabinet maker and leather
craftsman. Both woodwork and brass are often lacquered
and, because the equipment was usually well looked after,
the only deterioration is likely to be through dust. Use a
vacuum cleaner fitted with the fine nozzle covered with net,
or brush with a soft brush. Artist's sable paintbrushes are
best for dusting lenses; clean them with Kodak Lens
Cleaner, available from photographic dealers.

Brass parts can be cleaned with a cotton bud moistened in
white spirit as long as this does not affect the varnish; do not
allow white spirit to come into contact with rubber parts. If
steel parts show signs of rust, clean them with a cotton bud
soaked in **rust remover** such as Renaissance De-corroder,
and then give them a wipe with sewing machine oil.

For cleaning and reviving leather bellows, the lubricant
WD40 is hard to beat. For normal maintenance and for
keeping leather cases in good condition use colourless dubbin or Pliantine. If the black Morocco leather has been badly
scuffed and shows grey, a coat of artist's Indian ink applied
with a watercolour brush, followed by leather dressing, will
restore the finish.

Superficial blemishes on wooden surfaces may be erased
by a reviver such as Topp's Scratch Cover; more serious
damage may call for repolishing and should be dealt with by
an expert. If the bellows become detached from metal parts,
use HMG or Thixofix (reversible with acetone) to glue them
back.

See also LEATHER.

CANEWORK

Caning with rattan, a type of palm grown in the Malay
peninsula, was introduced into Europe by the Dutch. It was
fashionable in England for the backs and seats of chairs

from about 1660; its use was widespread during the Victorian period.

Rattan for canework is split lengthways and woven with the shiny outer side uppermost. This forms a light but durable and dirt-repelling surface which grows darker and browner with age. When canework has to be replaced in antique furniture its new yellowness can be toned down with an appropriate toned **wood stain**, applied with a brush and wiped off with an old rag. Do not darken it too much.

Dirt can accumulate in the mesh of the weaving: scrub with a stiff bristle brush and warm soapy water. Ingrained grime may be shifted by wetting the canework with warm water and then dabbing on white baking powder with a paintbrush; allow to dry and then brush off. Finally, wash the canework in cold water and leave it in an airy place to dry.

Broken strands of canework can be repaired by sticking a bridging piece of new cane behind the break, using a PVA **adhesive**. Always look for woodworm and treat it if necessary.

If the canework has been varnished and the varnish is flaking, you may need to strip it down. Sometimes rubbing with steel wool will be effective, otherwise a **paint stripper** can be used. Take care not to get stripper on the framework, apart from where the cane passes through the frame holes. Wash thoroughly afterwards. If you do not want to revarnish the canework, brush it with **microcrystalline wax polish** for lustre and protection.

If your piece needs recaning, do not be nervous of undertaking the job yourself: both books and practical courses are available to help. Otherwise there are specialist caners who can do it. Consult the Rural Development Commission* or ask a dealer in antique chairs for a contact.

CARPETS AND RUGS

The main areas of antique rug and carpet production include Turkey, the Caucasus, Persia, Afghanistan, India and China; the most most famous European factories were the royal Savonnerie workshops in France which began in the seventeenth century, and the nineteenth-century manufactures of Brussels and Kidderminster.

Most traditional carpets and rugs have a knotted thread pile which can be formed in a number of ways; others, such as kilims and soumaks, are flat-woven, without knots. Machine-made nineteenth-century and later European carpets have their pile formed by the weave, also without knotting.

Wool is the most usual yarn, but silk, cotton, linen and hemp may also be used in carpet weaving. The number of knots to the square inch, which determines the fineness or coarseness of the work, is one of the factors to consider in evaluating a carpet, but the number of colours used, the interest of the composition, age, geography and condition all play their part. Variations in colour and shape do not diminish value. The most interesting carpets were made by

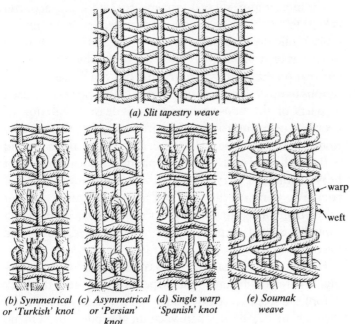

(a) Slit tapestry weave

(b) Symmetrical or 'Turkish' knot *(c) Asymmetrical or 'Persian' knot* *(d) Single warp 'Spanish' knot* *(e) Soumak weave*

←warp

↖weft

The principal carpet weaves and knots

nomadic tribespeople who may have had to dismantle and set up their looms many times during the manufacture of a single carpet; the wool may have been dyed at different times. The resulting imperfections are admired rather than criticized by collectors.

Having established that a carpet or rug is handmade, examine it carefully at the back for thin patches by holding it up to the light. Weak areas, old repairs and holes will be easily seen. The mending of holes and splits in the body of a carpet is a job best left to specialists, but simple repairs such as oversewing frayed edges to prevent them deteriorating further, or restoring tattered fringes, can be done with a stout needle and carefully matched yarn. Worn areas or weakened edges can be reinforced by stitching linen patches or bands of tape on the underside. Always sew repairs, never use adhesives on any part of a carpet.

The most important task is to ensure that the carpet or rug is kept in a suitable environment and cleaned from time to time. While the earliest carpets and rugs were used as table coverings or wall hangings, most are now subjected to wear and tear on the floor, where grit and dirt can cause the most serious damage. Try to ensure that valuable carpets are used in parts of the house where there is least circulation of people – in sitting-rooms or bedrooms rather than in corridors, for example. Use underlay, turn them round periodically and protect them by padding the legs and feet of heavy furniture. Very precious carpets and rugs should of course be hung on the wall and not walked over. Do not keep them in damp or very dry conditions, or in direct sunlight. Stored carpets should not be folded, but rolled over tubing with the pile outwards.

For day-to-day cleaning there is no substitute for vacuuming. Where possible, turn the carpet over and clean the back before the front to remove dust and grit that have filtered through to the floor, then vacuum the pile side. On no account take an old or valuable rug and shake it while

CERAMICS

holding one end or the side: this subjects the warp (foundation) threads to excessive strain. You can tap the carpet gently after draping it over a line, but do not beat it hard.

It is generally unwise to wash an old carpet or rug without the advice of a specialist, but if you decide on such an undertaking, make a preliminary test to find out if the colours are fast. Thoroughly wet a small section and then rub with a clean white cloth: if any dye comes off on the cloth, consult an expert rather than attempt cleaning yourself.

Localized soiling of carpets should be treated as soon as possible. Wet stains such as wine should be pressed with a clean cloth or kitchen paper to soak up as much liquid as possible and then sprinkled liberally with salt: leave this on until dry and then vacuum. Tackle grease spots with fuller's earth or french chalk: dust the powder over the affected area and leave for twenty-four hours; brush away and then vacuum clean.

Wax can be removed by placing blotting paper or kitchen paper underneath and on top of the carpet and ironing the spot with a warm iron; repeat with clean paper until no more wax appears. Spilt adhesives can sometimes be removed with white spirit which softens them enough to be pulled off in rubbery lumps. Remove chewing gum by hardening it with ice inside a polythene bag until you can scrape it off with a blunt knife.

See also TEXTILES.

CERAMICS

All ceramics are made of various types of clay, fired in a kiln, and most have a glazed surface. True porcelain, or hard-paste, was developed in China from the seventh or eighth century AD. Fired at a high temperature, it is hard, translucent and resonant when tapped. Soft-paste porcelains were the result of attempts to imitate Chinese porcelain (mainly in eighteenth-century Europe). Made from a variety of materials, they were fired at lower temperatures and are

41

both rare and delicate. Bone china, developed by Josiah Spode in the late eighteenth century, includes bone ash with china clay and china stone. Less hard than true porcelain, but translucent and more robust than soft-paste, this became the standard English porcelain body from the nineteenth century onwards.

Among the many pottery bodies, earthenware was and is the most widely used. Fired at a relatively low temperature, it is porous, opaque and less robust than porcelain; if chipped or cracked it easily becomes discoloured from the penetration of stains and water. Stoneware is a harder body, much favoured by studio potters, and usually heat resistant.

As most colours will not survive firing at the extremely high temperatures used to produce porcelain and bone china, they are often applied after the glaze has been fired. This means that care must be taken not to damage or rub off the decoration when cleaning badly stained items. Do not wash them in the dishwasher or use abrasives. A gentle washing in warm soapy water should be enough; rinse and dry carefully, with a cloth or (for encrusted or elaborately moulded pieces) a hairdrier set at cool.

Even this treatment is too much for soft-paste porcelains, gilded pieces or unglazed wares like terracotta, which must not be immersed. Swab them with cotton wool damped in soapy water or just dust with a soft brush. Ormolu or other metal-mounted ceramics must also be cleaned with great care: the metalwork must not be allowed to get wet. Cotton wool swabs damped in a fifty per cent solution of white spirit and water mixed with one teaspoonful of Fairy Liquid per pint can be used.

Biscuit and parian ware can be washed in warm soapy water, but if very dirty they can be cleaned with a mild **abrasive** such as Prelim or Solvol Autosol applied with an artist's stencil brush. Clean off with cotton wool swabs soaked in white spirit. This is also a good treatment for very grimy tiles.

42

Badly stained items such as teapots in practical use can sometimes be cleaned with a 20-volume solution of hydrogen peroxide or a mild solution of bleach: Steradent denture cleaner is effective and safer than most. Do not use bleaches on precious china or anywhere near painted decoration.

Broken china that is rare and valuable should have the attention of a professional restorer. If you are carrying out your own repairs to ornamental pieces, use a slow-setting epoxy resin **adhesive** such as Araldite. This is reversible with acetone or Nitromors (paint it on very carefully over the break, without getting it on enamelled decoration), and can be painted. It is not suitable for objects subjected to practical use (and washing up), for which old-fashioned rivets are the most robust solution. Superglues should only be used for wares of low value and are in any case not resilient to regular washing up.

Before undertaking any repairs, release old or badly executed mends by soaking in hot water, dabbing with acetone or painting with Nitromors (in the green tin) over the damaged areas. To remove rivets, which are made of lead, file through the centre and then pull the ends out with a pair of strong tweezers. Clean off all vestiges of dirt and old glue to allow a perfect fit. Prepare a means of support for the joined pieces while the glue sets: plasticine or masking tape can be used for this. Follow the directions for the adhesive, using as little as possible, and remove any surplus from the bonded edges straight away.

Chips or missing pieces can be modelled in epoxy resin **filler** (Sylmasta or Milliput) or in Araldite mixed with kaolin, titanium white or talcum powder. Add colour pigments to match the paste of the original china. Chemical Metal is another alternative which dries slightly softer than Araldite and can be rubbed down easily. Colour in any missing parts of the design with acrylic paints and then protect the surface with Rustin's plastic coating (either white or clear).

CHANDELIERS

Ornate hanging light fixtures, originally for candles but now usually converted to electricity, were designed to reflect the maximum amount of light with their glittering glass drops and beads. They are usually suspended from the ceiling, exposed to smoke, dust and other floating debris, and need regular cleaning. This is best done at ground level, and a large chandelier should always be installed on some kind of pulley system to enable it to be let down periodically.

Make sure the chandelier is disconnected from the electricity supply before you start, and then clean each section with swabs soaked in soapy water, taking care not to wet the metal framework nor to drop water down hollow branches; rinse and dry thoroughly, if necessary with a hairdrier set to cool.

If more radical cleaning is called for, you can dismantle the whole chandelier, but if it is a complicated structure, take a photograph first as a guide to reconstruction. Check the electrical wiring and the ceiling fixture. Metal connecting links should be opened sideways to minimize distortion. The separate glass drops, prisms and lustres can be washed in soapy water, rinsed and dried. Make sure every part is really dry before reassembling. Rubbing each glass piece wearing a pair of chamois leather gloves can enhance the sparkle.

Deteriorated metal parts and connecting chains and ties should be replaced. Use wire of the same colour as the original, whether this is silver, copper or brass: do not use steel wire as this can rust and stain the crystals. If glass elements are missing or broken you may be able to find suitable replacements in antique shops or good lighting suppliers such as Christopher Wray's Lighting Emporium.*

See also GLASS.

CHROMIUM

This bright shiny metal, plated on to base metals and plastics, has been used throughout the twentieth century on cars and bicycles, but also for decorative purposes, particularly during the Art Deco period. It scratches easily so it should only be cleaned with mild **abrasives** like Prelim or Solvol Autosol, or with soapy water: make sure it is thoroughly dried afterwards.

Air bubbles between the chromium plating and the base metal, and the subsequent corrosion of the base metal, can cause unsightly blackening pimples in the surface. These can be mitigated but not cured by polishing with Solvol Autosol and by keeping the surface dry. Small repairs can be made with Araldite.

CLOCKS

The amount of cleaning and renovation of clocks that you undertake depends on your own expertise with delicate machinery. For the conservation of clock cases refer to the FURNITURE section. Clocks dating from the fifteenth and sixteenth centuries are very rare, while those of the late seventeenth and early eighteenth centuries are particularly valuable. Antique clocks fall into two main categories: those driven by weights and those driven by a spring. Both types may have a pendulum for time-keeping, while carriage clocks and some mantel clocks have a balance wheel.

The grandfather or long-case clock is the best known of the pendulum clocks. Most were built in the eighteenth and nineteenth centuries and the basic mechanism is simple and robust. Some clocks go for thirty hours on a winding, while others run for eight days. In most instances the long case contains either one weight (thirty hours) or two (eight days). In the former the weight operates both hands and striking mechanism and in the latter there is a weight for each function.

To reveal the movement, remove the hood by releasing any catches and sliding the top section containing the glass door forward. In rare cases the hood may lift off. The main purpose of the hood is to protect the movement from dust,

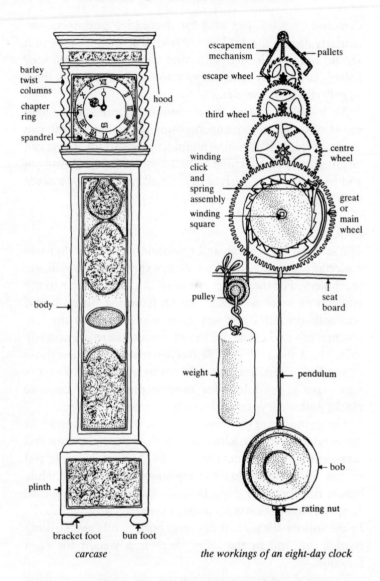

carcase

the workings of an eight-day clock

for it is this above all else that causes wear and damage. Never oil a dirty clock: wear residue and dust combine with the lubricating oil on the moving parts to make an abrasive paste that wears away the bearings, wheels and pinions. Dust, together with damp which causes mould or corrosion, are the clock's great enemies. Cleaning and oiling a clock is a specialist's job, and should be done every five years or sooner if the clock is in an unusually warm, dry or dusty place. Do not oil a clock yourself, especially with spray-based oils, and never use metal polish on any part of a clock.

Different clocks have different ways of obtaining an even beat. They will not function correctly if they are not properly set up, although they do not necessarily have to be exactly level. When setting a pendulum clock in motion you can hear from the tick if it is standing properly: an uneven beat indicates that the clock is not correctly positioned. All clocks should be placed out of direct sunlight, away from sources of heat and not in a position where they are liable to be knocked. It is advisable to secure long-case clocks to the wall to avoid accidents. This also ensures that when floors are being cleaned or polished the clock is not moved.

Pendulum clocks are regulated by lengthening or shortening the pendulum with a regulating nut below, above or in the middle of the disc-shaped weight or pendulum bob. Shortening the pendulum makes the clock go faster; lengthening slows it down. When lengthening it, make sure that the bob drops down to follow the nut.

Allowing a dead-beat escapement clock to unwind fully can be damaging to the movement if the pendulum swings with no power. When winding a thirty-hour clock by pulling up the weight by rope or chain, support the weight with your free hand, as it helps to reduce wear; do not let it bang the seat board (the base board of the movement) as it rises to the top. Wind key-wound clocks slowly and evenly until the spring feels tight but not forced: it should not be wound to its limit. Always use well-fitting keys to wind clocks.

To set the hands push only the minute hand slowly forward; if the clock strikes, stop and allow it to finish before moving the hand again. If the hands seem to be sticking, move the minute hand backwards one or two minutes (but not past a time when the clock should strike). At the same time encourage the strike to run by lightly pulling down the strike weight (generally on the left-hand side). If this does not free the hands, or if the minute hand does not move backwards, do not force it but seek expert help.

If the striking mechanism is out of step with the hands, it usually means that the locking plate or count wheel, a brass disc with slots in it, has got out of synchronization with the hands. This is corrected by moving the hour hand to the hour the strike is indicating. Repeat the process until strike and hands are in agreement.

All pendulum clocks should be moved as slowly as possible. Damage can be caused by the pendulum over-swinging. If you have to move a clock any distance you must secure the pendulum first. For this purpose most bracket and mantel clocks have either a hook or clip on the back-plate, or a block into which the pendulum can be screwed with a special knob; this is usually screwed into one of the case brackets when not in use.

Before moving a long-case, lantern or other weight-driven clock, remove the pendulum altogether. First slide off the hood, and dismount the pendulum by carefully unhooking it: the top of the pendulum rod is joined to a length of flat spring with a block of metal fixed to the other end. This is the feather or suspension and it is hung in a slit in such a way that the pendulum swings back and forth in the crutch which in turn is driven by the anchor-like rocking escapement; it can be easily damaged. Having removed the pendulum, you must also unhook the weights from their pulley.

A long-case clock must have its movement removed too. First lever the seat board off the case stands and lift the movement, with its seat board, free of the case. For travelling, pack it carefully in a close-fitting box, taking care not to damage the hands or the crutch at the back of the clock.

COINS AND MEDALS

Whether or not you clean coins depends on what you are going to do with them. If you are a coin or medal collector, you will know that the rule is don't clean them, as cleaning drastically reduces their value. If the coins are in mint or near mint condition, or are of significant value, you should handle them by grasping the edges or by picking them up with plastic tweezers.

If, on the other hand, you are going to use some coins of little value for decorative purposes, such as bracelets, pendants or a wall plaque, you may want to shine them up. Gold coins do not tarnish, so just wash them in warm water and dry them on a soft washleather. Silver coins can be brightened up with Silver Dip or with a **solvent** such as carbon tetrachloride applied on a cotton wool swab and then washed thoroughly and dried.

Old copper coins can be dipped (for a few seconds only) into a five or ten per cent solution of nitric acid and then rinsed thoroughly in a basin of water. Too long exposure to the acid will etch the surface, so great care must be taken. You can also use Silver Dip on copper coins. To keep coins bright and untarnished for long periods, buff them up with a wax polish or Long Term Silver Polish.

If you find ancient coins which have been buried or hidden, take them to your nearest museum without attempting to clean them in any way. The curator will give you professional advice.

CORAL

Coral is the skeleton of tiny marine animals and usually ranges in colour from deep terracotta pink to almost white; rare varieties include browns and black. For centuries, its branching structure has been exploited for jewellery, or it has been carved into ornaments, beads or encrustations for furniture and decorative objects. However used, it is characterized by a rich lustrous finish. Imitation coral, made from plastic, can be deceptive.

Clean coral first by dusting with a brush and then, if necessary, with a cotton bud or artist's paintbrush soaked in soapy water. Rinse and dry carefully; this can be done with a hairdrier on cool. It is best not to immerse coral in water. Persistent grime or a dull, scratched surface can be treated with a mild **abrasive** such as jeweller's rouge, Prelim or Solvol Autosol on a cotton bud. A final polish with **microcrystalline wax** should restore the lustre and protect the surface.

Repairs should be made with easily reversible **adhesives** such as HMG, Bostik or UHU All Purpose.

DOLLS

Dolls have been made from numerous different materials – wood, glazed porcelain, bisque, papier mâché, composition, wax, celluloid, plastic and fabric. Many have heads and bodies of different materials. Before carrying out any cleaning or conservation it is important to establish precisely which materials you are dealing with, and never attempt any but the most conservative procedures. The repair and conservation of dolls is a highly specialized business: dolls of any period may be very valuable and can be seriously damaged by improper treatment or unskilled repairs. If in any doubt, take professional advice. Dolls' hospitals such as Recollect Studios* will undertake repairs and supply missing parts such as limbs, eyes and wigs to match your treasure.

Wooden dolls may be of great antiquity. Their heads are likely to be covered in a layer of gesso, painted and varnished, and they should not be washed: dust with a soft brush, taking great care not to lift any loose paint. Composition and papier mâché dolls present similar problems and should be treated in the same way. They are likely to be very fragile: do not be tempted to restore them yourself.

Glazed porcelain, bisque and parian heads can be cleaned

with cotton wool swabs soaked in soapy water, taking care not to wet composition, leather or fabric bodies. Do not scrub, and be extra careful around the eyes and eyelashes.

Wax or wax-over-composition dolls must be treated with particular care and kept in cool conditions: they can easily be chipped or rubbed, and if subjected to even moderate heat they will soften and eventually melt. Remove any surface dirt with cosmetic cleansing cream on a pad of cotton wool, but do not attempt more radical cleaning or repairs yourself.

Celluloid and plastics can be wiped with a cloth or swabs soaked in soapy water. Celluloid is thin and dents easily, and is very difficult to repair. A highly inflammable material, it should not be given to children.

Fabric dolls, and particularly those with felt faces, should not be washed and are difficult to clean successfully. Confine your efforts to gentle brushing.

Dolls' bodies are less likely to be dirty than their heads, which is just as well since cleaning them can present many problems. Both composition and kid (leather) should be left well alone, and never cleaned with water. Fabric bodies can only be washed (in warm soapy water) if all the stuffing is first removed. Those with separate china heads and shoulders sewn on through holes in the shoulder plate should be detached first. Later the body will have to be restuffed, either with the original material carefully preserved, or with a suitable new stuffing.

Repairs should always be carried out using reversible methods. Broken china heads are extremely difficult to repair satisfactorily as their shape changes when the ceramic tension is released upon breakage. It is advisable to seek professional help, but should you decide to attempt such a major repair yourself, use a fast-setting epoxy resin **adhesive** such as Araldite Rapid or a quick-drying PVA such as Bison Extra Wood Glue and work from front to back of the head so that any mismatched fragments or botched areas (and there are likely to be some if it is a bad break) can be concealed more easily. Support your work on a fine sand or damp clay bed, and rub the repaired areas down to a smooth finish with fine abrasive paper. If whole areas are missing you can stick a piece of card or buckram to the inside of the head and then use an epoxy putty such as Sylmasta or Milliput as a filler. Small chips can be filled with PVA glue tinted with watercolour.

Many china-headed dolls have composition or 'pot' bodies and some dolls, made from the 1930s to the 1950s, also have heads made of this material, which takes a variety of different forms. These are easier to repair successfully than china heads. If you are repairing bodies (or heads) made of composition, use an epoxy adhesive. Missing parts can be modelled in epoxy putty (see CERAMICS) or Metalux wood filler. Small parts like fingers should be supported on an armature of florist's wire secured with superglue. Larger parts like hands or legs may need to be dowelled on. Insert a short length of thin wooden dowelling into the remaining part of the limb, if necessary embedding it in epoxy putty, and then model the new part using the dowel as a rigid base. Soft carvable balsa wood (from modelling shops) can also provide a suitable base for modelled replacement parts.

Restoring the colour on repairs to china or composition dolls is often the most difficult part, and it is important to carry out preliminary tests on an unobtrusive area to discover the most appropriate course of action. For major repairs you may need to use an oil-based matt paint like those made by Humbrol, applied with an air brush, but small areas can be touched in with watercolour or acrylic on a paintbrush. Never use cellulose-based colour or household paints.

Holes in leather and fabric bodies can often be patched by sewing on a piece of similar material. If you need to add filling, use the same sort of material as the original.

The segmented bodies of bisque-headed dolls most commonly suffer from perished elastic, and restringing them is

How a doll's limbs are strung

not a difficult job. The special round elastic used for the purpose is available from Recollect Studios*. Obviously the joints of the doll need to be in sound condition if they are to withstand the tension of the new elastic. They should be repaired before restringing, by a professional if the joint needs to be completely renewed.

Less radical joint repairs can be made with a paste of powdered papier mâché egg cartons (whisk them in a coffee grinder) mixed with a quick-setting epoxy adhesive. Work the socket into its round shape with a circular drill bit on an electric drill used at a slow speed (do not wear loose clothing for this task – it can be dangerous). Alternatively, joint sockets can sometimes be strengthened by flooding them with a thin superglue (Zap).

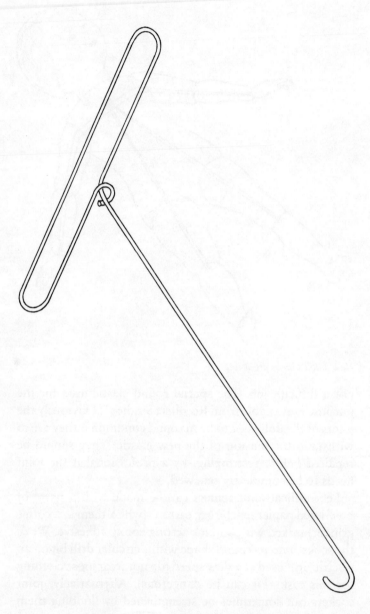

Homemade wire implement for restringing dolls

Once you have made sure that all the joints are sound, you are ready to restring the doll. Be careful as you unhook the old elastic: it may be under tension in parts of the body and suddenly releasing it could be damaging to the doll or to your own eyes. You will need to make a bodkin-like tool from a piece of fairly rigid wire (12 gauge) to facilitate the threading of the limbs together (see p. 54). Follow the path of the elastic as shown in the diagram on p. 53, or an alternative you may have noted on removing the old elastic.

The extremity of each limb is fitted with a hook or loop: supporting the head on a pillow, pass one double length of elastic up each arm and across the shoulders, hooking it at both wrists, then attach the head and finally the legs. This is done by passing another double length of elastic down the body and hooking it to the knees before bringing it up to the neck where all the knotted ends come together.

It is important to get the right tension: too tight stringing will cause friction to the limb and neck sockets, while too loose will result in a lolling head and floppy limbs. You will be surprised how much tension is needed to string even a moderate-sized doll.

Before about 1870, dolls were made with fixed eyes, either painted or of glass. Later, 'sleeping' dolls with counterbalanced eyes were introduced. In these, the two glass eyes are wired together and held in place in plaster sockets. A lead weight on a short rigid spindle is attached to the connecting wire at right angles so that, as the doll is lowered on to its back, or sat up, the weight opens or closes the eyes. To prevent scratching, and as a lubricant, the eyes were dipped into melted wax; this wax was also used to fix the eyelashes in place. Most china dolls' heads have a large hole in the top which provides access for adjusting or repairing the eye mechanism; it is usually covered by a cardboard, cork or composition dome, with the hair on top.

Dolls' hair ranged from a single hank glued into a slit on the top of the head to a full wig, glued to a removable dome

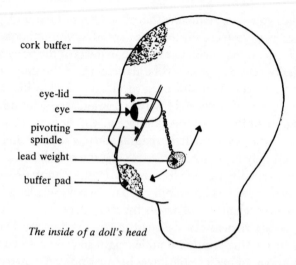

cork buffer

eye-lid

eye

pivotting
spindle

lead weight

buffer pad

The inside of a doll's head

of strawboard or composition. All kinds of animal, human and synthetic hair were used, and if you have to replace any, it is important to achieve as close a match as possible with the original. Do not be dismayed if you are faced with replacing the original hair with a completely new wig: modern reproduction dolls' wigs can be perfectly acceptable.

More often, the problem is one of tangling and dirt. First, untangle the hair, a little at a time, starting at the ends and taking care not to pull out or break the hairs. For dirty hair, dry shampooing is a safer alternative to washing in water. Use magnesium carbonate or a proprietary dry shampoo, or apply heated bran to the hair, working it in with the fingertips and leaving for five minutes before brushing out. A solution of Woolite, used to damp-wash the hair, can have good results. This process may soften the glue, which should harden again when the hair dries, but take care not to wet the glue too much or the wig will become unstuck. If appropriate, dress the hair as closely as possible to the fashions at the period of the doll's manufacture.

Whenever possible, the original clothes of an old doll

should be preserved, no matter how tatty they are. Follow the guidelines on the cleaning and care of TEXTILES. If new clothes are called for, make them as far as possible in a style contemporary with the doll; fashion plates of the period can provide useful guidance. Appropriate old materials can be used as long as they are in good condition, while new ones must be chosen with care and synthetics avoided.

DOLLS' HOUSES

If you are lucky enough to own or to acquire an old dolls' house, do not be tempted to 'restore' it, and do not allow small children to play with it unsupervised. It is a precious object and it should be preserved in as nearly original a condition as possible. As far as renovating is concerned, it is better to do nothing than to do too much.

Clean old paintwork instead of repainting it, and clean rather than renew old wall or floor coverings. Where parts are missing, replace and finish them to blend with the rest of the house. Loose or damaged parts should be glued back together again and any visible signs of the repairs carefully concealed by touching up with paint or whatever finish is appropriate.

Dirt may have become ingrained while a dolls' house has stood in an attic or store. Remove superficial dust and then carefully wash away the tenacious grime with **non-ionic detergent** or Fairy Liquid and warm water, working on a small area at a time and drying it before moving on. Be careful not to soak off any papers or decorations. Treat any evidence of woodworm, and repair damaged parts with PVA **adhesive**, making sure you clean out all perished glue first; if a **filler** is needed, use animal glue and sawdust, Milliput or original interior Polyfilla.

Do not over-clean mellow old paintwork and if retouching is essential, use carefully matched poster paints. These are opaque and fill up cracks if applied thickly. Slightly dilute and apply with a small flat brush, then brush out to give a smooth finish. If a gloss finish is required, use one coat of retouching **varnish**.

The scale of most dolls' houses is one inch to the foot, but other reductions were also used, and these may pose problems if you are buying antique dolls' house furniture. There is now a flourishing trade in both new and old furnishings for dolls' houses, and no shortage of books to help those wanting to make their own.

ENAMELS

Enamelling is the process by which sheets of metal are coated with powdered glass of different colours and fired in a kiln. The technique has been used for decorative purposes since ancient times and takes several different forms. The most important are *cloisonné* (enclosed), in which the coloured enamel is contained within strips of metal soldered to the base; *champlevé* (raised field), in which the base itself is incised or cast with depressions to hold the enamel; *basse taille*, a development of *champlevé* in which the enamel is applied over a gold or silver background chased in low relief; *plique à jour*, a type of *cloisonné* without the backing, so the enamel is transparent like a stained glass window; *guilloché*, in which an engine-turned surface is covered with enamel to create translucent patterns; and painted, in which the metal is not part of the design but merely provides the backing for it.

Ideally, enamels should only be dusted with a soft brush; if this is not enough, clean them with swabs of cotton wool damped in soapy water, rinse with clean swabs and allow to dry thoroughly. Damaged enamels should be cleaned with cotton wool buds damped with acetone or carbon tetrachloride. Never immerse enamels in water, and avoid using cloths for dusting as they can catch raised or damaged areas.

All enamel is very brittle, and can suffer from stresses resulting from uneven expansion rates in the metal backing and the glassy decoration; a knock can shatter the surface. Damage may take the form of crazing, cracking or chipping of the enamel decoration, while the backing, which may be of silver, gold, copper or bronze, is subject to the particular problems associated with those metals.

Chips of enamel can be replaced using an **adhesive** such as HMG, Bostik or UHU All Purpose. While restoration of serious casualties involves re-enamelling (and refiring) by a specialist enamel restorer (a porcelain restorer will sometimes tackle the work), small areas of damage can be cosmetically (and reversibly) remedied at home. Use acrylic paints, which have enough body to build up the surface to the right thickness, as well as allowing missing parts of the design to be reinstated. To protect restoration of this type, and to consolidate flaking or fragile areas, a coating of retouching **varnish** is a good idea.

FANS

There are basically two types of fan – rigid and folding: it is the semicircular folding variety that is the more collected and more often in need of attention. Typically, the pleated mount is supported by about sixteen or eighteen flat sticks with a guard stick at each end; these are united at the base by a central spindle, often with a ring for carrying the fan when closed. A *brisé* fan is one without a mount: the sticks themselves, usually pierced and joined by interlaced ribbon, form the fan.

The sticks of a fan may be of wood, tortoiseshell, horn, ivory, bone or mother-of-pearl, while fan leaves are as diverse: silk, lace, feathers, paper, parchment, calfskin (sometimes known as chicken skin) are among the most usual materials. They can be decorated with embroidery, painting, piercing or carving, lacquer, piqué work, jewels or spangles.

With so many materials and decorative techniques involved in their making, fans can present diverse problems.

Obviously it is important to observe the principles of care for the particular material concerned. Fans should be stored either in their folded state, if possible in their original boxes but at least wrapped in acid-free tissue paper, or in a loosely open position well supported with acid-free tissue or polyester wadding. Never display them in sunlight or without a protective glazed case; open and close them as rarely as possible.

If cleaning is essential, follow the guidelines for materials such as lace and silk (see TEXTILES), tortoiseshell, ivory and mother-of-pearl. Paper, parchment and leather fans may be cleaned very carefully with a spotlessly clean artist's eraser or Draft Clean, but do not rub hard, especially over painted decoration, and do not use breadcrumbs as they may leave fatty deposits.

The ribbon in a *brisé* fan may have rotted: this can be replaced, using a new one as close as possible to the original, and following its system. This is not always as easy as it appears, especially if the fan has only one slit in each stick; three-slit sticks are easier to rethread. Always clean off old glue before you begin.

For the three-slit type, measure a length of ribbon slightly longer than the width of the open fan and, with the front of the fan facing you, attach it to the inside of the right-hand guard, using HMG or PVA **adhesive**. Thread the ribbon from front to back through the first slit and continue backwards and forwards through every slit, always passing the ribbon from front to back of the first slit in each stick, and making sure that every stick slightly overlaps the one behind it. When you have got to the end, check that the tension is even and allows the fan to open and close before gluing the ribbon to the back of the left-hand guard.

For single-slit *brisé* fans you need a short length of ribbon for each stick, plus two extra ones: cut them the length of two stick widths. Working from right to left with the fan facing you, glue the first ribbon to the inside of the guard (with HMG or PVA); the second ribbon to the front of the first stick, the third ribbon to the front of the second stick, and so on to the opposite end of the fan. Then come back to the right-hand guard and thread the ribbon attached to it and the ribbon attached to the first stick through the first slit from front to back; glue the first ribbon (from the guard) to the back of the first stick and trim if off; bring the second ribbon forward, threading it and the third ribbon through the slot in the second stick; glue the second ribbon at the back. Continue in this way, keeping the sticks slightly and evenly overlapping, until you reach the end.

Broken sticks can sometimes be mended with glue (animal glue for wood, PVA or HMG for other materials) if there is a large enough area of contact. Otherwise a splint of a suitable material will be needed. A strip of veneer can be used for a wooden stick, while a sliver of bone or even plastic would be suitable for ivory or tortoiseshell: stain them to the right colour. Once the repair has set hard, trim the splint down to the right shape and smooth off the edges.

If the rivet holding the sticks at the bottom of the fan is broken it should be replaced or mended: if the fan sticks are allowed to hang free the mount will be strained and easily damaged.

Fans of the rigid or screen type, often of painted wood or papier mâché, are usually supported on the thinnest of carved or turned handles: these tend to break, especially around the point where they join the screen. If they cannot be satisfactorily reglued (with animal glue), a new handle may have to be made and attached. A friendly turner may be able to provide a suitably fine turning; the top end needs to have a groove into which the fan leaf is fixed, generally with a minute screw.

When in doubt, seek professional help. The Fan Museum* has a resident conservator who can give advice or undertake repairs; it will also supply parts such as rivets and suitable ribbon without selvage for rethreading brisé fans.

FRAMES

Neglected wall fixtures and picture hangers are the main cause of damage to picture and mirror frames: cords rot, wires perish, screw eyes and rings rust and pull out of their holes, and wall fixings may be inadequate. Check all these from time to time and replace as necessary.

No repairs to frames should be undertaken until pictures and glass or mirrors have been removed. The most common problem is failure of the corner joints. Make sure the right angles of the frame are square, either with a set-square or with an accurate right-angled piece of wood or hardboard, and then reglue them with PVA **adhesive**. If necessary reinforce the join by driving two or more panel pins diagonally through the sides of the frame to hold the two corners together. With larger frames, substitute wooden dowels for the pins, or screw metal corner plates on to the back of the frame if you are sure the frame is strong enough to carry them.

Some frames are extremely fragile, and wooden fretwork or carving can snap off. You may need to cut and fit new pieces to replace missing parts. Whenever possible use wood of the same variety and texture as the original and cut a paper pattern from the corresponding part on the opposite side of the frame as a guide. If the frame is not thick enough for a simple glue joint to hold, reinforce the back with a strip of thick veneer.

Natural wood frames and most painted frames can be cleaned by a gentle wipe with a damp cloth once the loose dust and cobwebs have been brushed off. Apply a coat of **microcrystalline wax** as a protective finish. Treat mahogany and maple frames like polished furniture; they should not be wetted, nor should they be stripped and repolished unless the original finish has deteriorated beyond resurrection.

See also FURNITURE, GESSO and GILDING.

FURNITURE

In the normal course of its life old furniture suffers a great deal of wear and tear; in addition it may be subjected to stress or accident, central heating, clumsy repair or injudicious restoration. It is important that any procedures you embark upon will not add to these problems, and will neither shorten the useful life of venerable pieces nor devalue them. Do not be afraid to tackle basic repairs, but carry them out sensitively and with due respect for authenticity. Use animal glue for all the repairs listed here unless another adhesive is specified, and do not be tempted to reinforce a glue joint with nails, screws, brackets or other devices, all of which tend to weaken rather than strengthen the repair. Always leave radical procedures, or restoration of valuable items, to a competent restorer.

Furniture is particularly vulnerable to fluctuations in temperature and humidity and is most often damaged by over-indulgence in central heating: try to balance your own comfort with that of your furniture, and at least use some form of **humidification** if the atmosphere is dry. Good maintenance should also include carrying out minor repairs before they become major ones, vigilance for woodworm, fungal attack or other pests (and treatment when necessary), and regular dusting.

In cleaning and polishing furniture do not be over-zealous, and try to preserve original finishes whenever possible. Repolishing should only be undertaken in extreme circumstances: the accumulated wax and dirt of ages help to form the patina, and even scratches and inkstains are part of an object's history. Do not attempt to make your antiques look new.

Arming yourself with general knowledge about antique furniture is the first step in competent care. There are many good books to guide you through period styles, the principles of proportion, the kinds of timbers used at different periods and in different places, the types of furniture made through the ages and their methods of construction. In addition, try to spend some time looking at, and if possible handling, examples of old furniture in museums, dealers' showrooms and auctioneers' salerooms.

Beading, moulding and stringing
Beadings are thin strips of wood that are applied to furniture, either for decoration or to cover up joints; mouldings are used in the same way but are usually made from compound shapes and are sometimes carved; and stringing consists of fine inlaid lines of wood, metal, bone or other material. They are particularly vulnerable to catching on clothing or dusters and often lift if subjected to fluctuations in temperature and humidity. It is wise to hold any breakages or damage in place with a gentle adhesive tape like low tack masking tape until you have time to make a permanent repair or can take the piece to a restorer.

Cock beads are the small projecting beads round the

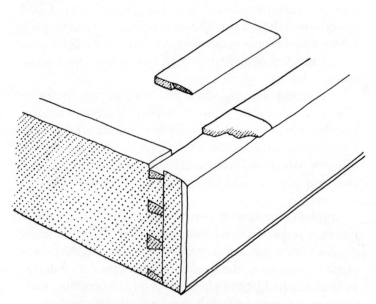

Cock bead repair: cut away the jagged edge with a neat straight line and insert a new piece

edges of drawer fronts. They were in use from the eighteenth century, and are particularly prone to damage. They are secured in channels cut into the sides and bottom of the drawers and across the full depth of the top edge. Cock beadings of various sizes are available from some timber merchants but they are also very easy to make. Most wood suppliers will run off a few metres of rectangular wood of suitable dimensions: all you have to do is round the forward edge with sandpaper.

When replacing cock beads, first decide whether to replace the whole length or only part of it. In cases where the damage is extensive, it is better to replace the whole side, while small repairs can be spliced in. Cut out the broken section; corner replacements will need mitring (that is, ensuring that the angle is 45 degrees) to fit. The new section should be secured with animal glue (and veneer pins if necessary) and held in position until completely dry (about twenty-four hours). This should be done by placing waxed paper over the repaired area and then applying pressure in the form of a weight, clamp or rubber bands: the inner tubes of old tyres, cut into strips, are good for this purpose. Finally, smooth down with a block plane and sandpaper to make an invisible repair and finish by polishing to match as nearly as possible the rest of the piece (see FURNITURE *Polishing*).

If you need to repair damaged moulding it is unlikely that you will be able to buy a length to match from a timber merchant or DIY shop, so you will probably have to make it yourself: this is not a difficult task, and in most cases only a few inches are required. First, prepare the broken area by making all the edges square and clean. If a section of beading has been shattered or broken off, make a diagonal cut with a small hand saw right through the moulding, taking care not to cut into the carcase. Clean the area thoroughly with a chisel, making sure that all the old glue is removed and the surface is absolutely flat.

If the damaged area is in the centre of the beading or a section of a radius (like a piece on the edge of a pie-crust table), make the aperture wedge-shaped, so that a new section will slide into place until it makes a tight fit without any gap. Do not attempt to shape the piece used for the repair before gluing it into place; just fit it to the surfaces that are going to be glued to make a perfect joint, leaving a generous overhang all round, to be planed and filed down after fixing. Try to select a new piece from wood similar to the original moulding, and place it with the grain running in the same direction. Once the glue is hard you can shape it. Simple beadings and mouldings can be finished merely with a plane and sandpaper, but for more intricate ones you will need gouges and carving tools.

Stringing lines that have become detached or lost can be replaced by gluing them into their original channels; it is

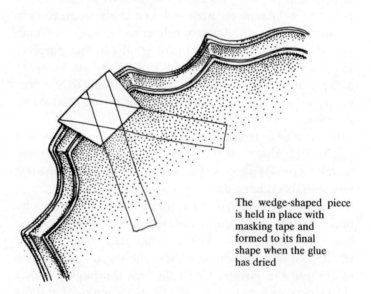

The wedge-shaped piece is held in place with masking tape and formed to its final shape when the glue has dried

Repairing a pie crust table

66

important to clean out thoroughly all the old glue and accumulated dust before attempting this. Metal stringing that has lifted and buckled may have to be cut and flattened before being reglued into position. This requires considerable skill and is best left to a professional restorer.

Bruises and dents

Bruises and dents in wood can sometimes be reduced by placing a pad of wet tissue or muslin on the affected part for a day or two: this will cause the fibres of the wood to swell. The advantage of reducing a dent in this way must be weighed against the disadvantage of damaging the surface finish which is likely to result from treatment of polished or painted furniture.

Castors

Where wood has been cut away or has rotted to such an extent that original fittings such as castors can no longer be held on securely, pack the enlarged cavity with a **filler** such as sawdust and animal glue before replacing the castor.

Drawer runners

If you look at the front of a chest of drawers and notice that the drawers are tipping slightly backwards, this is almost certainly because the runners are worn at the back and need replacing. Since the late seventeenth century drawers have been constructed so that they run on two strips of wood which are extensions of the sides. Depending on the weight of things in the drawers and the frequency of their opening and closing, these runners wear down and at the same time cut channels in the dust boards. The rate of wear on drawer runners can be reduced considerably if they are rubbed with the butt of a tallow candle about once a year. This lubricating coat of wax reduces the friction and makes the drawers run more easily.

Replacing runners is, properly speaking, a job for a

professional; short cuts, such as gluing new runners next to the old worn runners, tend to widen the area of potential damage and may produce more problems for the future. If you must pursue this course, however, do not use nails for fixing new runners: wear and tear on the wood means that nail heads will eventually stick out and could wreck the dust board.

Drawer stops

Some drawers are prevented from sliding too far into the body of a piece of furniture by small blocks of wood fixed to the dust boards. These stops, subjected to hard wear, can be knocked off or become so badly worn that the drawer overrides them. The positioning of new stops is critical, and measuring, rather than guesswork, will prevent frustration. Use a marking gauge, if you have one. Measure the thickness of the drawer front and transfer this measurement to the place where the new stop is to be fitted, then glue and pin it into position, making sure you punch the pinheads below the surface of the stop or they will wear through the drawer bottom.

Feet and legs

The feet of furniture are obviously vulnerable to damage from damp, whether from rising damp or frequent floor washing, as well as from woodworm and rot. It is important at the outset to treat the cause of the problem, and to ensure that the feet are thoroughly dry before attempting any repairs. If at all possible, avoid replacing them: regluing and pinning may be all that is necessary. Rickety bracket feet can be reinforced by gluing a wood support to the back. If you have to replace a foot, make it a fraction longer than the others and then sand it down.

When chair or table legs are of uneven length, rather than cutting the long legs down, which can be disastrous, build up the short one by gluing a slip of hardwood on to it and then sanding it down until the piece stands firmly.

Breaks which are clean and new can often be repaired simply by gluing with animal glue, but anything more complicated should be dealt with by a professional restorer.

Handles
If you cannot find antique brass fittings to replace missing or broken ones, you will have to use reproductions. Try to match the originals as closely as possible. If you have reason to believe that the handles or knobs on a piece of furniture are unsuitable later replacements, you should study good examples of the appropriate style and period before choosing fittings, which will have a crucial influence on the character of the whole piece.

Hinges
Hinges often work loose because their screw holes have become enlarged or the wood around them has split. Sometimes old handmade screws, because of their shallow pitch, become embedded in the surrounding wood and will no longer unscrew. These must be drawn out like nails (see also SCREWS).

Enlarged screw holes can be plugged with tapered slivers of softwood, glued in place; cut the ends off flush with the surface with a sharp chisel. Make a new hole to start the screw with a bradawl, and replace the hinge with the correct size of screw: its head should fit flush into the countersunk screw hole. Too large a screw will stand proud and place stress on the hinge and the surrounding wood; one that is too small will work loose in no time.

When the wood around a hinge is split and cannot be glued back in place, a new piece should be inlaid. This must be solid enough to bear the pressure of the screws and hinge.

Inlays and intarsia
Furniture may be decorated by inlaying contrasting coloured woods or other materials such as bone, ivory, mother-

of-pearl or metal into cavities cut into the solid surface. Intarsia work is an elaborate, usually pictorial, form of inlaid decoration. Both must be dusted with great care to avoid lifting loose or raised fragments of the design. Furniture decorated entirely with inlays of wood can be cleaned and polished in the same way as solid timber furniture, but inlays of other materials must obviously be treated appropriately.

When pieces of inlay become detached, try to reglue them in place (with animal glue) as soon as possible, before they get lost; if they are missing, you can probably match in fragments of a similar tone and cut them to the right shape. In either case, make sure you clean out all old adhesives before refilling cavities.

Marquetry and parquetry

Decoration made from combinations of different shapes and colours of veneer applied to furniture surfaces reached its peak as an art form during the eighteenth century, when fine furniture was veneered with all kinds of naturalistic designs or stylized borders and motifs in a wide variety of woods; parquetry is the term used for geometric marquetry patterns.

In order to achieve perfect results, several sheets of variously coloured veneers were glued together, interleaved with sheets of coarse 'sugar' paper. The design was then fretted out of the laminated sheets with a special saw and then each was separated and washed clean. At this stage shading of the design with hot sand would have been carried out. The completed picture would be assembled and held together with a sheet of paper stuck to the face before being glued permanently on to the furniture carcase. Once it was attached, the paper could be removed and final details of the design filled in.

Marquetry can be cleaned in the same way as ordinary furniture. Loose parts should be carefully detached, cleaned of all old glue and stuck back into place with animal glue (see also *Veneering*). Replace missing sections with wood of suitable variety and colour, if necessary using a **wood stain** to achieve the correct tone. Make a paper pattern of the missing area by covering it with a sheet of paper and taking a pencil rubbing. Cut out the resulting pattern and stick it on to a suitable piece of veneer; adjust it to make a perfect fit by sanding the edges as necessary, and then glue it into place. If appropriate, add additional detail with Indian ink or fine felt-tip pen, but try to carry out such restorations in gentle tones or they will stand out too obviously against the mellow original. It is a wise precaution to practise on another surface first!

Painted furniture
Painted finishes on furniture were much more common than surviving examples would suggest. Largely because of the fashion for stripped pine which began in the 1960s, huge quantities of interesting but unpretentious furniture has been subjected to stripping in caustic soda, with the result that many attractive pieces have lost their original finish and with it their unique character. If you come across furniture with a painted finish, resist the temptation to strip it.

Some early paintwork, especially in country districts, was done with milk paint, a resilient liquid consisting of boiled-down buttermilk and pigment with or without animal blood. The type without animal blood appears as a cream or grey finish on cottage furniture. It can be brightened up with one or two coats of powdered skimmed milk mixed with water to the consistency of emulsion paint.

Stable painted surfaces can be cleaned with swabs damped in soapy water, but first make sure that the paintwork is not flaky or likely to be damaged by this treatment; different coloured pigments can react differently from each other. Rinse the soapy mixture off carefully and when the surface is dry, give it a coating of **microcrystalline wax** for protection and lustre.

If you suspect that an original painted or gilded finish survives beneath another layer or layers, you should try to establish the paint history of the piece before deciding how to proceed, however humble you think it is. This involves taking samples from the paint layers and having them analysed; the conservation department of your local museum should be able to help. New techniques are being developed for cleaning painted surfaces with enzyme gels (ask the Victoria & Albert Museum's Conservation Department for details), but dry stripping is something you can do yourself. Chipping away the surface layers very carefully with a round-edged copper or brass scraper, pieces of glass or coins requires patience rather than ingenuity, but can be rewarding. The alternative, stripping with Nitromors, will almost certainly cause damage to the original paintwork or gilding you are trying to save, however carefully it is done.

If you are stripping paint or varnish with the intention of revealing the wood beneath, use a **paint stripper** and follow the advice on page 168.

Polishing

On early furniture, beeswax was the usual polish base and there is nothing better than a pure wax finish built up over many decades. The seventeenth- and eighteenth-century alternatives were methylated spirit-based shellac varnishes or oil-based varnishes.

French polishing, which involves laying on successive coats of shellac dissolved in methylated spirits, was introduced into Britain during the early nineteenth century. Its mirror-like 'piano finish' pleased the Victorians so much that they consigned large quantities of eighteenth-century and earlier furniture to be french polished, and often stained with the new aniline dyes into the bargain. Such inappropriate treatment still persists. The twentieth century has given us cellulose and other synthetic finishes applied with a spray gun. Do not be tempted to use them on your antique furniture.

For general maintenance of waxed furniture, use a solid polish containing a high proportion of beeswax or **microcrystalline wax polish**. While you can make up your own (see **furniture polishes**), it is easier to use one of the many proprietary brands recommended for antique furniture. They are produced in a range of colours from neutral to dark brown, so you should be able to select a matching tone. Furniture wax will also help to conceal the odd scratch, but for this you may find an appropriate coloured wax **filler** (Liberon) or even boot polish more effective. Some furniture creams contain emulsifying agents which will dissolve wax and damage the surface patina, so they are best avoided; never use aerosol polishes or those containing silicone.

Polishing once or twice a year is enough. The wax should be applied on a soft cloth and rubbed in with a circular movement; polish it off with a clean lint-free cloth before it has become dry and hard. Leaving it on too long will result in streakiness. Apply wax to carved furniture with a short-haired paintbrush or a shoe brush and work it well in. It can be burnished off either with a brush or a soft cloth. Do not allow polish to come into contact with gilding or ormolu, but it is a useful protection for brass handles. French polished furniture should be dusted only, not waxed.

Dull and grimy waxed surfaces can be revived by rubbing down with fine steel wool (oooo grade) lubricated with wax polish; go with the grain and rub evenly.

While the Victorian brilliance of **french polish** built up by applying dozens of coats of shellac is no longer fashionable, it is usual to apply a few coats to fill, but not conceal, the grain of the timber as a basis for wax polishing. French polishing is a highly skilled process, so do not expect perfect results if you attempt it yourself. The transparent type of french polish available from DIY merchants is probably your best choice.

French polishing

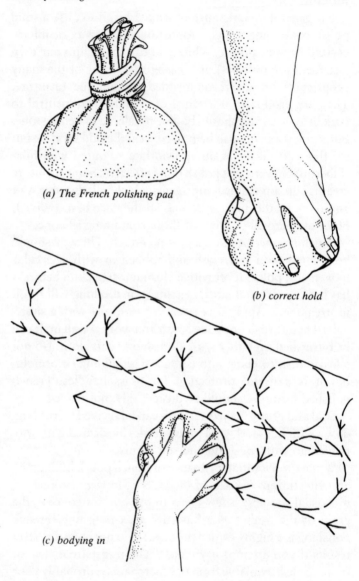

(a) The French polishing pad

(b) correct hold

(c) bodying in

Before applying any french polish, examine the piece of furniture very carefully. Make sure it is entirely free of dust and dirt. Success depends on a perfect foundation, so time spent at this stage will bring rewards later. The room in which you are working should be both dust-free and warm – at least 60°F (16°C); in cold temperatures french polish tends to bloom and turn milky. Protect your hands with a barrier cream or wear disposable surgical gloves.

Make a polishing pad (known as a 'rubber') out of a piece of upholsterer's wadding about 7–10 inches square, folding it first into a triangle and then turning the corners in to produce a ball. Place this pad in a square of lint-free cotton rag, giving the ends a twist so that they are held in the palm of the hand out of the way. Extend your fingers and grasp the pad with your fingertips. Practise this before wetting the pad with polish. The rag holds the pad together and keeps fluff from the wadding away from the surface when polishing. By increasing or decreasing the pressure of your fingers, you will regulate the flow of the polish to the face of the rubber. Now unfold the rag and moisten the wadding with methylated spirit. Place the opened triangle of wadding on the rag in the centre of your outstretched palm. Wet the wadding liberally with french polish, fold in the corners and fold up into a ball as described previously. Squeeze any excess polish out of the rubber by pressing it lightly on to a piece of card or old board.

Apply the liquid methodically in a series of tight circular movements, each one overlapping the last. As the polish dries almost instantly, apply successive coats immediately. Take care to ensure that no blobs or dribbles are left; go back immediately to mop up any surplus polish on the surface.

On most furniture timbers, three or four coats are sufficient for surface sealing, but apply as many coats as you need for the required depth of polish. After a maximum of about a dozen coats, let the work stand for a while to harden before sanding over lightly with **garnet** or **Lubrasil paper** (9/0 or 320 grit).

Next, using a drier and firmer pad which will leave no wet patches or ridges of polish, apply another coat of polish with long graceful strokes of even weight. Vary the place where the pad comes into contact with the surface on every stroke, and continue the sweep beyond the end of the polished area. Wherever possible, polish in the same direction as the grain. Once you are satisfied, set the work aside for at least three hours, during which time the surface will consolidate and harden.

At this stage you will see that the surface is shiny and brash: Liberon Burnishing Cream gives the work a mellowness and depth while imparting added hardness. Shake the container thoroughly and then wet a pad of cotton wool generously with the cream. Taking one manageable strip at a time, polish up and down the grain about twenty times over, exerting pressure. While each section is still moist, polish it with a clean duster until the surface is dry: this completes the process.

Rings and stains
The three commonest causes of rings and stains on the surface of polished furniture are heat, alcohol and water. Unfortunately there is no magic wand that can eradicate them, and success in removing them depends on the degree of penetration into the layers of polish. Treatments are generally a combination of frictional heat, mild abrasives and lubricants. Old remedies which may be effective include cigarette or cigar ash mixed with saliva, rubbed into the blemish with a finger covered in a clean cotton rag; and camphorated, linseed or olive oil mixed with a mild **abrasive** such as fine pumice powder. Brass and silver polishes sometimes work, but they must be used with caution as they contain wood alcohol which dissolves french polish. Commercial remedies such as Topp's Ring-

away will be effective if the damage is not too deep.

Persistent stains such as ink or ball-point pen are almost impossible to remove without repolishing. A bleach such as oxalic acid (see **Bleaching agents**) can be used, but its effect is difficult to control on a limited area and it may have to be applied over the whole surface. If you do use oxalic acid, rub it on with Scotchbrite rather than wire wool: the latter can cause combustion in combination with oxalic acid. In any case, marks should be left alone unless they are very unsightly: they are signs of age and use, and part of the history of an object. Removing them can easily detract from its character and value.

Splits, cracks and holes

For small cracks on the surface of well-patinated old furniture, a hard wax **filler** (Liberon) is the kindest repair material. More structural cracks can sometimes be glued and then pulled together with a sash cramp. Larger splits due to shrinkage should be filled with slivers of wood tapered to the shape of the gap; these should be glued, cramped and, once dry, planed and smoothed to the level of the surrounding timber.

Holes and other sorts of damage are best repaired with a stopper made from fine sawdust of the same wood as the furniture mixed with just enough animal glue to bind it together without making it soft or wet. Press it into the hole or crack and, once it is hard, it can be levelled with a chisel or a plane and then polished to match its surroundings. For those wanting a short cut, there is Brummer stopper, which comes in various colours.

Staining and colouring

Furniture finishes should look as natural as possible, and antiques should have the warm sheen produced by generations of waxing and care. The process of staining is one of the most subtle operations in furniture renovation and requires much experience to perfect. As a general rule, the less stain that is used on antique furniture the better. Wood colourants fall into two main types: the traditional stains usually applied in water-based solutions and those dissolved in spirits or naphtha (see **Wood stains**). The latter are easier to use, but have a tendency to fade and alter unpredictably.

Apply stains with a cotton-wool pad to ensure an even distribution, and do not try to achieve the desired tone in one or two applications. Build the colour by starting with a light shade and gradually applying darker colours. Certain woods used for inlays and stringing, such as boxwood and holly, are virtually impervious to stains at normal dilutions. If you do need to colour these woods, concentrated solutions of stains will be needed.

If you need to bleach wood, for example to match a repair to faded mahogany, oxalic acid or hydrogen peroxide are recommended. Special wood-bleaching chemicals are available from wood finishing suppliers, but they are drastic in their action and must be used with extreme care (see **Bleaching agents**).

Veneers

Veneers are thin sheets of wood, usually of interesting figuring, which are stuck with glue to the outer surfaces of a piece of furniture made from less expensive wood. The technique provides opportunities for showy effects, while allowing economy in the use of precious timbers; it was developed in England from the second half of the seventeenth century.

Before the advent of power-driven machinery in the nineteenth century, veneers were cut by hand sawing; up to eight sheets could be obtained from an inch of timber, and there could be variations in thickness over a single sheet of veneer. Machine-cut veneers, produced from the Victorian period onwards, are considerably thinner and more regular in thickness.

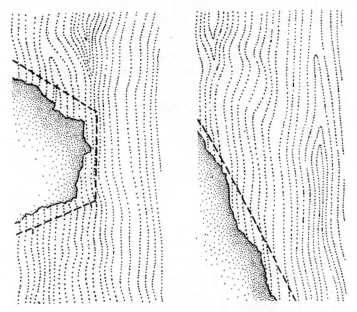

Veneering: cut out a suitably shaped area with smooth sides

Because the characteristics of antique veneers are so different from those of today, you will avoid extra work if you preserve broken pieces and glue them back in place as soon as possible – before they are lost. Should a piece of veneer be missing, you are faced with finding a suitable replacement. Most professional restorers cut their own veneers to obtain a good match of both grain and colour, so a local restorer's workshop would be a good place to try; otherwise *Yellow Pages* may produce the name of a veneer merchant or woodworking supplier who can help you.

You may have to use thinner veneers for your repairs than those originally used. In this case, laminate two or even three layers together. Always try to use a veneer thicker than the original: after the glue has set, the new piece can be planed and sanded down to the correct height.

When repairing broken and jagged areas, cut away the uneven edges with a sharp, thin-bladed knife such as a

Stanley knife; follow the pattern of the grain wherever possible. When you have to cut across the grain, make your cut curved rather than straight as this will make the finished repair less noticeable. If you are repairing cross-bandings on the edge of a piece of furniture, make your cuts divergent or wedge shaped rather than parallel: this will ensure a neater fit.

Next, carefully clean away all old glue and dirt from the repair area. This can usually be done by scraping with a chisel blade, but you may have to wash away persistent glue. Then make a paper pattern of the required shape by placing a piece of paper over the area and lightly rubbing over the surface with a lead pencil to produce an outline of the cavity. Cut your pattern with a pair of scissors and fit it into the cavity to ensure that it fits perfectly. Glue this pattern on to a suitable piece of veneer and cut out the shape with a sharp knife, undercutting the joining edges very slightly to leave a small surplus on the overhanging edge. With the paper pattern uppermost, fit the new piece, adjusting it, where necessary, with fine sandpaper held flat on a cork or wood block. When you are sure it fits, glue it into place. The paper pattern need not be removed until the glue has hardened. If you do not have animal glue, a PVA **adhesive** is suitable. Hold the repair firmly in place with masking tape or, if it is a big repair, clamp it until the glue is thoroughly dry.

Bubbles and blisters in veneers are caused by variations in movement between the carcase wood and the veneer, usually as a result of extreme fluctuations in temperature or moisture. If you tap with your fingernails on suspect surfaces, you will hear a hollow sound where veneers have broken free. Old and perished glue can often be revived and the loose areas stuck back again by applying a damp cloth to the area and pressing it with a hot iron. This treatment is likely to destroy the surface polish, which will have to be replaced.

Sometimes the bubbles are so badly distorted or the

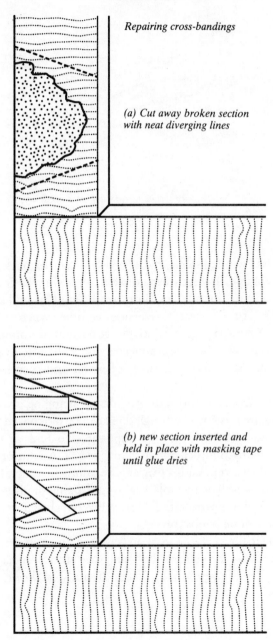

Repairing cross-bandings

(a) Cut away broken section
with neat diverging lines

(b) new section inserted and
held in place with masking tape
until glue dries

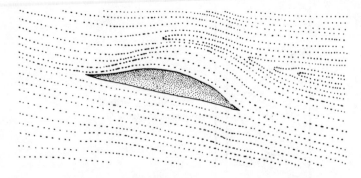

Treating a veneer bubble: slice through, work in glue if necessary, and iron down

veneer has swollen so much that it will not shrink back to its original shape. In this case make a cut, following the grain of the wood, for the full length of the blister. This will allow one edge of the veneer to override the other when ironing down. Where the glue is so far gone that it cannot be revitalized, introduce new adhesive under the lifted veneer with a palette knife or a sliver of wood and then iron it down.

On occasions, sections of ornamental stringing or cross-banding are missing. Although these can be purchased from veneer merchants, it may be impossible to find an exact match for anything other than plain borders. A solution is to replace the section with a piece of sycamore or similar light-coloured wood of suitable grain, and paint or draw the pattern to the appropriate colour. When polished over, such a repair will be almost invisible.

Paint strippers can be used on veneered furniture without risk of lifting the veneers, but take care if the veneers are already loose. Keep broken pieces carefully so they can be replaced.

Warping

One of the most difficult problems to remedy is the warping of table tops, bureau fronts, cupboard doors and other large areas through changes in the moisture content of the wood: central heating is the most usual culprit. Attempts at repair through steaming and wetting will produce only temporary results, and it is best to seek professional help.

GESSO AND COMPO

Gesso is a paste made of whiting or chalk mixed with glue. It has a long tradition of use in providing a smooth base for decoration or gilding. Composition or compo, its thicker and more glutinous cousin, is made from plaster of Paris and animal glue, and is used for moulding and for modelling details such as flowers and figures on frames, often on a wire armature. Gesso is used in a thin gruel consistency as a grain filler on wood, and slightly thicker as a base for painting or gilding; mixed to a paste it can be used to fill in missing detail and to form low relief decoration.

To make gesso, take animal glue in jelly form, cut it into small pieces and put them in a container; just cover them with cold water. Place the container in a saucepan of boiling water and when the glue has melted, mix it and remove from the heat. Slake handfuls of powdered whiting into the glue until the sedimented whiting lies just below the surface of the glue. Mix again and keep it warm and melted but not hot. To make a thinner gesso solution, add twice as much water to the glue before heating it.

Broken or missing areas of gesso can be built up with successive coats applied with a brush; allow each coat to dry before applying the next. When the gesso has reached the right height, allow it to dry completely and then rub it down with fine garnet paper (see **abrasives**) to form a smooth marble-like finish. Finally, burnish it with a damp cloth.

Where old gesso has become detached from the base woodwork through shrinkage, new gesso paste can be worked in underneath with a palette knife; cracks can be filled the same way. If large areas are to be restored, the gesso should be scraped down with a square-edged steel scraper. At all times the surfaces should be wiped free of dust with a damp cloth: this applies to partly completed work as well as to old damaged surfaces.

Should areas of compo be loose on the surface of a frame, dilute PVA **adhesive** with a touch of water so that the glue becomes thin enough to spread evenly over it with a soft paintbrush; check that there are no dribbles. This will dry off to secure the existing compo and to give a sound structure for any repairs to mouldings or decoration.

To make compo, heat animal glue to melt it and then let it cool to body temperature before gradually adding plaster of Paris and stirring to eliminate lumps. You may need to put it through a fine sieve at this stage. The mixture should have the consistency of whipped cream. Formerly, compo was shaped in carved wooden moulds which required great skill to prepare. The need for these has now been superseded by synthetic rubbers and materials such as dental alginate which allow casts to be made from existing decoration quite easily (see **Casting and modelling materials**). Replacement decoration can also be made with Das clay mixed with PVA adhesive: this is an ideal material for hand-moulding.

Once made, the new mouldings can be glued to the object with HMG or PVA adhesive and details of the decoration carved in as necessary.

GILDING

Gold leaf can be applied to mirrors, picture frames and furniture, either entirely or partially, when it is known as parcel gilding. Gilded surfaces are fragile, vulnerable to changes in relative humidity and easily chipped or rubbed. Gilding can be laid on a carved wood base on gesso, or over moulded composition. A coating of gesso on top of the carving or moulding provides a smooth keying surface for the gold leaf, while a layer of colour known as bole (usually deep red or yellow) forms a cushion for the gilding. The gilding itself may be water or oil gilding, and it is difficult to distinguish them. Water will destroy water gilding, while white spirit and other solvents will damage oil gilding, so unless you know what sort of gilding you are dealing with do not be tempted to clean it with anything more drastic than a soft brush to remove dust.

Do not try to restore worn gilding. If parts of a gilded frame are missing, they can be recarved in wood or re-moulded (see **Casting and modelling materials**); chips can be repaired with a **filler** such as Das modelling clay and PVA or interior Polyfilla and, once dry, rubbed down with fine wet and dry paper.

For touching up minor repairs (or for cheap frames) you can use a gilding wax such as Rowney's Goldfinger, Reeves's Restoration Wax, Winsor & Newton's Treasure Wax or Liberon's Gilt Cream (Chantilly is the best colour to use in most instances). Match the colour carefully and if necessary prepare the surface with an appropriately tinted watercolour or poster paint, normally yellow with red highlights. Apply the gilding wax with a finger or with a piece of rag; buff with a soft brush to give a lustre and, if necessary, 'distress' the gilding back to show a hint of the coloured undercoat. Gold paints are not advisable except for cheap frames as they tend to have a dull lifeless texture and they make future restoration more difficult. The best one available is Winsor & Newton's Treasure Liquid Leaf. Protect these finishes with a coat of clear **varnish** (from art shops).

The intrepid and deft may care to attempt oil gilding; the technique is as follows. First carry out any necessary repairs and rub them down so that they are perfectly smooth. Buff the whole surface with 0000 wire wool. Paint the correct colour undercoat, again usually yellow with red highlights, and when it is thoroughly dry apply either four-hour gold size or Japan gold size. Allow this coat to dry to a tacky stage. The art is to catch the gold size at just the right time. Test it with the back of your hand: it should be only slightly tacky. If it is too dry the gold leaf will not adhere, and if too wet the leaf will cockle up and wrinkle.

The easiest gold leaf to use is either transfer gold or Schlag (Dutch metal in loose leaf form). The former comes in books of twenty-five 2 × 3 inch sheets, each lightly held by wax on a piece of tissue paper for convenient handling, while Schlag is supplied in 500-leaf batches and can be picked up with the hands (unlike real gold). The leaves should be applied directly to the tacky surface with a strong brush to drive them home. Each should slightly overlap the preceding one, with every join in the same direction. Rubbing in the direction of the overlaps, brush down the whole area to produce an evenly covered surface; vacuum it and then polish with **microcrystalline wax**. If you are using Schlag you should apply a protective coating of Jenkins' Hot Colourless Lacquer (HCL Jo71 – from gilding suppliers) to prevent discoloration.

Single sheet oil gilding cannot be burnished, but a good match to properly burnished work can be produced by double thickness gilding. To do this apply a thin coat of wax polish to the newly gilded surface as soon as it has been laid and buff it lightly with a soft shoe brush. As soon as the wax is barely dry apply a second coat of gold leaf; this will adhere to the tacky wax. Burnish it with a stiff bristle brush or, if you have one, an agate burnisher.

Gold leaf borders on leather desk tops and book bindings are transferred from a gold strip with a heated brass wheel engraved with a continuous design.

Gold leaf illumination and gold figures are produced by painting the design required in Japan gold size and pressing a sheet of transfer gold on to the sticky surface. The gold leaf will only adhere permanently to the tacky size.

GLASS

Glass is produced by the fusion at high temperatures of sand or flint with a flux such as soda, potash or lead; limestone is sometimes added. Different oxides introduced into the raw materials produce glass of varying properties, qualities and colours. In its molten state glass can be blown, drawn, moulded or pressed into shapes; when cool it can be cut, etched, polished or painted.

Crystal glass contains various proportions of lead oxide which makes it sparkle. The best lead crystal, containing twenty-four per cent lead, reflects all the colours of the rainbow when correctly cut and has a pure metallic ring when struck. It should not be confused with rock crystal, which is a much-prized natural material found in different parts of the world.

Because nearly all glass is brittle and easily broken, cleaning must be done with great care. Normally a washing in warm water with a mild liquid detergent is sufficient. Do not use very hot water, as violent changes in temperature can cause some glass to crack. Drain on a soft surface like a tea towel or kitchen paper to avoid scratching the edge of the glass, and then dry with a linen cloth; a final polish with a chamois leather is a good idea. If a piece of glass is very dirty or thick with dust, it is not advisable to clean it without washing: dry dusting can cause minute scratches on the surface. Never put old or valuable glass in a dishwasher.

Iridescence on glass that has been buried is a form of decay of the surface. It is part of the object itself and should never be cleaned off ancient glass. Less precious objects such as bottles from Victorian rubbish tips can be washed with warm water to which a little water softener and biological washing powder have been added. If possible, avoid removing any labels that survive.

Chinese glass snuff bottles should never be washed as they may be painted inside with unfired pigments which can be destroyed by water. Damaged 'weeping' or crizzled glass,

glass with ormolu mounts, and items with rubbed or unstable gilding or enamel painting should not be immersed either. The colour on some 'stained' glass, particularly of the Victorian period, is easily removed with water, so clean carefully with cotton wool swabs damped with soapy water, and stop at once if the colour seems to be unstable. Leaded glass must also be cleaned carefully to avoid getting water behind the lead.

Persistent stains such as hard water deposits, wine and chemical stains will need stronger treatment than just washing. The simplest treatment is to leave some colourless vinegar in the stained vessel for twenty-four hours and then rinse it out. If this does not work, try swilling the inside with warm water and a denture cleaner such as Steradent. Alternatively, dissolve a teaspoonful of a water softener such as Calgon in one pint of warm water and leave it in the vessel for twenty-four hours before rinsing. The old remedy of swilling the glass vessel with water and sharp sand or lead shot is likely to cause irreparable damage through scratching, and should not be tried. Commercial glass cleaners should only be used on utilitarian objects, not on antiques. Never use commercial window cleaners on stained glass or leaded windows.

Decanter and other glass stoppers should either be removed for long-term storage or smeared with Vaseline to prevent them sticking. If you come across a jammed stopper do not apply force but first warm the neck of the vessel to cause slight expansion; if this is not enough, introduce a little penetrating oil around the stopper. This should allow it to be gently twisted out. Alternatively, make up a solution of two parts of methylated spirit to one part of glycerine with a few camphor crystals (from the chemist) and allow it to penetrate the crack around the stopper for several hours before attempting to withdraw it.

Repairs to precious glass should only be undertaken by a conservator, but ornamental items that are not going to be used can be mended with a reversible **adhesive** such as HMG, Bostik or UHU All Purpose. Only use superglue for utilitarian pieces of negligible value.

Minor chips can sometimes be rubbed down with fine wet and dry emery paper. Fine **abrasives** such as jeweller's rouge or crocus powder can remove scratches, especially if applied (cautiously) on a rotating polishing mop on an electric drill.

HARDSTONES

Hardstones, or *pietre dure*, include agate, cornelian, jasper, onyx, chalcedony, lapis lazuli and other semi-precious substances used either on their own for vessels, boxes, jewels and all kinds of decorative items, or in combinations to form mosaic or naturalistic designs on the richest of furniture: most of this work was done in Italy.

Clean with cotton wool swabs damped in soapy water; rinse, dry and polish with **microcrystalline wax**. Repairs may be made with HMG, Bostik or UHU All Purpose clear **adhesives**.

HORN

A versatile and robust material, horn in one form or another has been used in the past for such objects as drinking vessels, gunpowder containers, musical instruments, lanterns, snuff and other small boxes, dressing-table accoutrements, spectacle frames and jewellery; it is still used for spoons. It can be steamed and moulded, carved and sliced: in thin sheets it is translucent.

Horn should not be immersed in water, but it can be cleaned with cotton wool swabs damped in **non-ionic detergent** and then rinsed with swabs or a cloth wetted in clean water; dry carefully with a cloth or, for intricately carved pieces, with a hairdrier. Do not wet painted horn, as the paint layer will be very vulnerable. Dulled, grimy or scratched surfaces of unpainted horn can be improved with a mild **abrasive** cleaner such as Prelim or Solvol Autosol and then an application of **microcrystalline wax polish**.

Small repairs can be made, or flaked and cracked areas stabilized, with PVA, UHU or Bostik All Purpose clear **adhesives**.

IRON AND STEEL

Iron may be cast or wrought. Cast iron contains up to five per cent carbon and is produced by pouring the molten metal into a mould. Traditionally it has been used for such objects as firebacks and fireplace surrounds, garden furniture (since the nineteenth century), ornaments such as doorstops and cooking pots. Cast iron cannot be forged and is virtually impossible to weld: composite pieces have to be bolted together. It is brittle and can break if dropped or carelessly used. Wrought iron has a much lower carbon content (about 0.5 per cent); it is ductile and can be worked into elaborate shapes. It has been used for ornamental gates, lanterns, fire-irons and all kinds of architectural features.

Steel is an alloy of iron and carbon with other metals; it can be polished to a brilliant shine and has been used since an early period for cutting implements, weapons and ornamental items. Stainless steel, a twentieth-century development, is non-rusting through the inclusion of chromium.

The chief problem with old iron and steel is their tendency to rust: cast iron is more prone to rusting than wrought iron. Serious and unchecked rusting will eventually lead to disintegration of the metal. For this reason objects of iron or steel should never be kept in a damp atmosphere, and their surfaces should be protected with wax, oil, graphite (black lead) or paint. They should be cleaned with methylated spirit rather than water.

Superficial rust spots can be cleaned with very fine wire wool or a nylon pot scourer moistened with a little oil. Steel can be cleaned with Prelim or Solvol Autosol applied in even strokes with a cotton wool swab. Finish by polishing with a soft cloth, taking care to remove all vestiges of the cleaning substance. This is most effective for steel-bladed knives, for example, but great care should be taken if the object is blued or damascened, inlaid with other metals (like Bidri ware), or decorated with engraving, gilding or with beads of cut steel. These can easily be damaged by over-enthusiastic cleaning or polishing. Always take rare or precious pieces to a conservator.

Before attempting to clean seriously rusty iron, make sure it is dry and then brush off all flaking paint and rust with a wire brush; if necessary, remove old paint with a **paint stripper** such as Nitromors, with a hot air paint stripper or with a blow-lamp. Remaining or less severe rust can be treated with a **rust remover** such as Jenolite or Modalene which contain rust inhibitors, or with Renaissance De-corroder. Paraffin is also effective: paint it over the surface and allow it to soak in for several hours before rubbing off with wire wool and then wiping with a cloth.

Once the object is clean and free of rust, it should be handled as little as possible (wear gloves to prevent finger-marks) before being protected in an appropriate manner. For cast iron fire-grates, stoves and other domestic items, black lead or Zebrite gives the best finish. Ornamental ironwork that is not in practical use can be protected with matt black paint. A light machine oil gives protection from rust but needs frequent renewal and never dries so is prob-ably useful only for items such as tools. A good natural finish on ornamental pieces can be obtained with **micro-crystalline wax polish**, while a coat of transparent lacquer or **varnish** gives a glossier protection. Ironwork that is kept outside should be painted regularly.

Small repairs can be carried out with epoxy resin **adhesive** or epoxy metal **fillers**, while broken wrought iron should be taken to a blacksmith.

IVORY, BONE AND ANTLER

Ivory includes not only elephant tusks, but the tusks and teeth of walrus, narwhal, hippopotamus and whale; vegetable ivory comes from the nut of a tropical palm. The importation of all animal ivory is now banned. Ivory is distinguishable from bone by its dense structure and gently striated appearance; it is an excellent carving material and polishes to a rich waxy lustre. Bone is lighter, whiter and more brittle, and has dark flecks on its surface.

Antler, generally rough and dark on the outer surface, is a form of bone from the outward growths on the skulls of various kinds of deer. Displayed antlers collect dust because they are usually placed out of reach. They should be vacuum cleaned and/or wiped with a soft cloth damped with methylated spirit. Polish the horns with wax polish. If the horns are joined and the boss is covered with fur or skin, this should be treated with moth-proofing from time to time.

Before the introduction of plastics, ivory was an important new material for the manufacture of a huge number of objects including knife and umbrella handles, billiard balls and gaming pieces, piano keys, decorative figures and jewellery; it was a favourite base for miniaturists, and much used for inlays in furniture and ornaments. Because of the high cost of ivory it has been widely faked, usually with plastics. Some of these 'ivorine' imitations are hard to detect without a microscope.

Among the most valuable bone objects are ship and other models made by French prisoners during the Napoleonic Wars, but lace bobbins, spoons, paper knives and other domestic and decorative items were made. Bone was also used for inlays, and particularly key escutcheons, on furniture. Antler has been used for buttons, knife handles, decorative objects and even furniture.

Ivory and bone are both vulnerable to changes in temperature and humidity, and can warp, split and crack if they become too dry. Objects should be kept in a coolish, dryish place, away from heaters, direct light and strongly coloured materials. Never immerse them in water, but clean by gently dusting with a soft brush and then, if necessary, wiping with a cotton bud or cotton wool swab damped in slightly soapy water. Rinse in the same way with clean buds or cotton wool and dry with a soft colourless cloth. Never use this damp treatment on painted or gilded ivory or bone, and never use bleaches.

Uncoloured ivory surfaces can benefit from treatment with almond oil. Paint it on with a fine brush until the whole surface looks oily; leave for about eight hours and then wipe away surplus oil with cotton wool swabs. **Microcrystalline wax polish** is also recommended.

Inlays of ivory or bone may have become darkened with a build-up of polish and dirt. They can be cleaned by carefully scraping with a cocktail stick followed by wiping with a cotton bud damped in white spirit: be careful not to dislodge the inlay or allow the spirit to attack the surrounding wood or other material.

Breaks in ivory or bone may be repaired with a reversible **adhesive** such as PVA, HMG, Bostik or UHU All Purpose adhesive. Cracks can be consolidated by immersing the object for about five minutes in molten candlewax tinted with titanium white to blend, and immediately wiping off the surplus. For valuable items seek the advice of a professional conservator before attempting repairs.

Ivory and bone knife handles in normal domestic use must be treated rather differently from decorative objects. They should be kept out of water as much as possible and they should never be put into a washing-up machine, but even with such care, the glue fixing the handle to the blade may deteriorate over the years and need to be replaced.

Having removed the blade from the handle, scrape out the old glue with a spike or skewer and wipe off the residue from the inside of the handle and the shaft of the blade with hot water and/or surgical spirit. Use epoxy resin adhesive to refix the blade in the handle.

JADE

Jade is a hard, brittle and translucent stone which may be of many colours from the most familiar shades of green to pink, white, yellow or black. Jadeite – more translucent and usually of a deeper emerald green – and nephrite are also classed as jade. Imitations are widespread, but genuine jade can be distinguished by its hardness and coldness to the touch: it can scratch glass. Especially valued as a carving material, it has been used predominantly by Chinese and Indian craftsmen.

Jade can be washed in soapy water. Polishing with micro-crystalline wax will revive and protect the surface. Small repairs can be carried out with HMG, UHU or Bostik All Purpose clear adhesive.

JET

A type of coal that can be carved and polished, jet was most fashionable for mourning jewellery during the Victorian period, but was also used for trinkets and souvenirs. It is sometimes hard to distinguish from imitations in black glass or synthetic materials.

Jet can be cleaned with cotton wool swabs or a soft brush moistened in soapy water, or with Prelim or Solvol Autosol, taking care to remove all traces. Polish with a soft cloth. Small repairs to clean breaks can be made with cyanoacrylate adhesive (superglue). Fill chips or missing areas by melting a drop or two of hard black wax (Liberon) into the cavity, allowing it to harden again, and then carving it to the required shape. Do not allow jet to come into contact with white spirit, acetone or other solvents.

JEWELLERY

Although jewellery, by definition, is designed to be worn, it is often made of vulnerable materials which need care in use and handling. The hardest gemstones, diamonds, for example, are liable to scratch other stones if they rub against them; rubies, sapphires and emeralds are brittle and can crack or even shatter if given a hard knock; opals, turquoise and many other opaque stones are porous and can be damaged by water; most stones are easily scratched, and some are damaged by ultra-violet light or by chemicals in perfume, make-up and hairsprays. Whenever possible, jewels should be kept in their own boxes, separate from others, or at least wrapped in acid-free tissue in a padded jewel case. Fastenings, links and hinges should always be checked before wearing, and thinning metal parts monitored: if necessary, take damaged items to a jeweller to be repaired.

All jewellery needs cleaning from time to time, to remove the accumulated deposits of dirt, dust and body oils which make it look dull and lifeless. Pieces with open-backed settings which do not involve porous stones, pearls or other materials damaged by water can be cleaned with a soft toothbrush in soapy water: use a small tray or dish covered with a cloth, or a special jar with a mesh dipping basket and allow the jewel to soak in the solution before brushing the dirt out of the crevices. Rinse in clean water and then leave it to dry before buffing with a soft cloth or chamois. For more thorough cleaning use a dip like Goddard's Jewellery Care before the washing process.

Jewellery with closed settings should not be immersed in water or dip, but should be cleaned with cotton wool buds damped with a solution of surgical spirit or brushed with a soft toothbrush wetted in mildly soapy water. Necklaces with threaded beads should not be immersed (see BEADS), nor should materials such as coral, ivory, tortoiseshell and enamel (see appropriate headings). Jewels containing porous or other non-wettable substances (opal, turquoise, marcasite, pearl and so on) can be cleaned with a jeweller's cloth or with powdered magnesium carbonate. Place them in a jar and cover them with the powder; shake gently and leave for several hours before removing and brushing off. Very grimy pieces can be cleaned with Prelim or Solvol Autosol: take care to remove all traces, if necessary with a cocktail stick (never with a pin), and then buff with a chamois leather or jeweller's cloth.

Repairs to valuable jewellery or the resetting of precious stones should always be carried out by a reputable jeweller, but there is no reason why costume jewellery should not be refurbished at home. Craft and bead shops supply a range of fittings and fastenings for necklaces, ear-rings and brooches which are useful for replacing broken ones. Detached stones can be glued back into their mounts with reversible PVA or non-reversible superglue: use a pair of tweezers and a magnifying glass to ensure accuracy. Metal pins and clasps, and broken glass beads or artificial stones, can also be fixed with superglue or epoxy resin **adhesives**. The latter are suitable for foil-backed settings where other glues might be visible.

LACQUER AND JAPANNING
True lacquer is the resinous sap of a tree that grows only in the Orient and it has been used to decorate furniture and small objects in China and Japan since ancient times. The surface is built up with as many as twenty or thirty coats of lacquer, usually coloured, and each rubbed down before the next is applied. The resulting hard lustrous finish may be carved, inlaid with mother-of-pearl or semi-precious materials, or decorated with painting and gilding, often in relief. Japanning, the European technique developed in the seventeenth century to imitate oriental lacquer with shellac or gum lac varnishes, may also have relief decoration.

Both oriental lacquer and European japanning can be damaged by light, heat and water, and are liable to crack and chip, especially if the underlying material is unstable. Dust them carefully, with regard for any loose flaking areas or chips: a soft brush may be more suitable than a duster which can catch on rough edges. Grimy surfaces can be cleaned with cotton wool swabs damped in a solution of warm water and Synperonic N, but test a small area first to make sure the decoration is not fugitive. Rinse with swabs damped in clean water and then swab dry. Dulled surfaces may be improved with a coat of **microcrystalline wax polish**.

Loose or flaking pieces can be secured with HMG, Bostik or UHU All Purpose clear **adhesive**, but more adventurous repairs to oriental lacquer are best left to a professional restorer. Japanned surfaces with damaged relief decoration in gesso can be restored with gesso or a **filler** such as interior Polyfilla or Das with PVA, and then rubbed down to a glassy smoothness before colouring with acrylic artist's paints or regilding. Finish with a single coat of clear **french polish** or with **microcrystalline wax polish**. Do not attempt such restoration on very valuable items, but take them to a professional lacquer restorer.

LANTERN SLIDES

Glass slides for magic lanterns, consisting of a positive image on a transparent base (not to be confused with glass negatives), are either photographically produced or made from transferred colour pictures. The photographic type, in use from the last quarter of the nineteenth century until the mid-twentieth, are usually 3 ¼ inches square. The image on the transferred type is protected by an extra sheet of glass, and the two pieces of glass are held together within a wooden frame or bound round the edges with passe-partout tape. Another type, of variable size, also within a wooden frame, may be hand-coloured and in consequence not very securely fixed. Many of these do not have a covering glass and so are particularly vulnerable.

Lantern slides should be stored in their own grooved cases or in boxes with separating slats; alternatively in individual polyester envelopes or wrapped in acid-free tissue; they should not be allowed to touch each other.

Brush away dirt and dust with a soft artist's brush. If more drastic cleaning is required, wipe the outer glass surface with a swab dampened with water and **non-ionic detergent**: never try to clean the surface to which the image is stuck. You may need to replace the passe-partout if it is damaged. This is difficult to find nowadays, and the best substitute is brown paper adhesive tape.

This is a soft heavy metal with a low melting point, and it has been used traditionally for casting and beating into garden figures, urns, cisterns, guttering, ornamental rain-water hoppers and coffins. Cutting it reveals a shiny surface, and when first cast it has a dark silvery sheen, but it soon weathers to a dull grey.

Because of its weight and softness lead is vulnerable to distortion, denting and scratching: large items like garden figures have to be supported inside with an armature of iron or steel, and if this fails the statue will eventually collapse. Lead is also subject to corrosion from other substances such as oak, sweet chestnut, chipboard, cardboard, household paint and vinegar, all of which give off acid fumes. The surface of corroded lead is white and powdery and the object becomes distorted; it should be wrapped in polythene and taken to a professional conservator.

Lead should be cleaned by swabbing with warm water and **non-ionic detergent** or, in the case of outside objects, with a soft bristle brush to remove dirt and bird-droppings. After cleaning, protect the surface with **microcrystalline wax polish** applied and burnished with a soft shoe brush.

Dents may be pushed out with a rubber hammer (a metal one will leave marks), but take care not to thin the metal and cause holes or tears. Splits and holes may be repaired by a good plumber or, in the case of precious pieces, a professional conservator of metalwork.

Always wash your hands after touching lead in any form. Corroded lead is particularly poisonous.

LEAD SOLDIERS

These are very collectable, but have often been played with until most of the original paint has been chipped and projecting parts such as limbs and guns have been bent or broken. There is not much you can do to repair breaks, and bent parts are likely to snap off if you try to straighten them. Whenever possible, leave the paintwork in its original state: repainted figures lose much of their value. However, there is little harm in renovating very distressed soldiers by repainting their original liveries. Use Humbrol enamels, sold in small pots by artists' and model-making suppliers.

Like other lead objects, model soldiers should be kept in acid-free conditions.

LEATHER

For centuries, leather has been used for upholstering furniture, covering trunks and boxes, binding books, making harness and for many other purposes. Although leather can perish or rot, good care and maintenance can keep it healthy over a long period. Check the framework of leather-covered objects for woodworm infestation, and treat if necessary. A pinkish or red powdery condition known as red rot can affect some leathers, causing irreversible damage. While there is not much you can do about this, you may consolidate generally roughened leather surfaces with an application of Pliantex (see **Leather treatments**).

Dust leather objects with a soft brush, a vacuum cleaner, or a photographer's puffer brush. Robust smooth-surfaced leathers can be cleaned with saddle soap, obtainable from leather shops or saddlers; test a small area first for colourfastness and suitability. Using a damp rather than a wet sponge, work the saddle soap into the surface with circular movements and then rinse with a clean damp sponge; once the leather is dry buff it gently with a soft cloth.

It is better to clean antique or fragile leathers with liquid potassium oleate soap (Vulpex) mixed with white spirit (one part of Vulpex to at least twenty parts of white spirit); apply carefully with a sponge or soft cloth and rinse off with another damped in clean white spirit.

Soft-surfaced leathers such as suede can be cleaned with powdered gum eraser (Draft Clean): rub it over the surface with your fingertips and then brush or vacuum it off. Proprietary suede cleaners may be used on modern suedes.

Old leather that has become parched and tired-looking can be revived and made more supple with a leather dressing. For robust items such as luggage you can use Connolly's Hide Food but the alternative, Pliantine, is good for nearly all leathers, including bookbindings.

Apply the dressings sparingly on a linen or cotton cloth, or with your finger, and follow the directions supplied. The special acrylic wax blend, SC6000, provides the best protective surface coating for leather, but **microcrystalline wax polish** can be used as an alternative.

Never wet or rub gold tooled decoration with cleaning substances or leather dressings.

Repairs to tears or splits in leather should be done from the back: use thin leather or canvas for thick leathers, and nylon net or silk for thin ones; hessian or canvas can be used for reinforcing fragile leather. Stick patches and reinforcements with PVA emulsion **adhesive.**

Where sewing is the best means of repair (threads are inclined to wear out more quickly than leather), use a waxed thread, or a strong button thread waxed with beeswax or a candle stub. Thread it with a needle at each end and, using the existing holes in the leather, start with the thread midway through one hole and proceed by passing both needles through the same holes from opposite sides. Continue thus in contrary motion until you have finished the repair.

Replacement leathers for tables and desks can be purchased from several specialists. Given the dimensions of a rectangular or square leather, or an accurate paper pattern

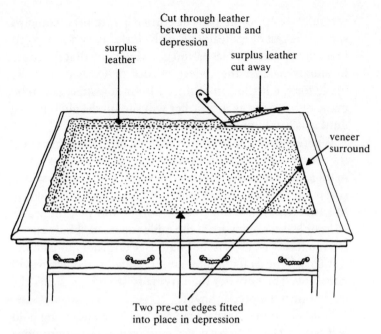

Cut through leather
between surround and
depression

surplus
leather

surplus leather
cut away

veneer
surround

Two pre-cut edges fitted
into place in depression

Recovering a leather desk top

of an irregular shape, such companies will produce a leather
to fit, complete with gold blocking and a 'blind edge' which
is a tooled pattern without gold round the perimeter of the
leather. The leather will be supplied with a selvage which
will eventually be cut off two adjoining sides.

Prepare the surface of the table or desk top by removing
every vestige of old covering and glue. This is best done by
wetting it and using a chisel-shaped paint or wallpaper
scraper. Leather is easily stretched out of shape, so do not
apply glue to the prepared leather, but only to the surface
where it is to lie. Use PVA **adhesive**, and if a large area is to
be covered, wet the surface with water first and then spread
the glue with a comb-edged spreader. An alternative method
is to use wallpaper adhesive, but as this is wet it tends to
cause the leather to stretch and bubble.

Having glued the whole surface, take the leather and

carefully position the pre-cut corner before proceeding to spread the rest of the leather little by little, using a soft rag to press out the air bubbles as you go. Make sure that the edges fit snugly against the veneer border or excavated recess made for the leather to fit into. Minor adjustments can be made quite easily as the leather will slip on the glue surface until it is firmly pressed down.

Where the selvage overlaps the sides, press the leather into the recess with a blunt tool such as a paper knife; this will mark a line where the leather is to be cut to fit. Do this with a sharp knife such as a Stanley knife, angling it slightly towards the rebate. Start in the corner and pull the waste strip of leather away from the table top as the blade cuts it free. In this way, even if the blind edge does not quite fit, the leather will be exactly right, and the small discrepancy will not show. This is better than trying to stretch or shrink the leather into the precise shape.

Gold decorated borders are applied by transferring gold leaf with a heated brass wheel engraved with a continuous pattern.

LOCKED DRAWERS
If you feel unwilling to call in a locksmith to unpick your lock with skeleton keys (which can be expensive), there are various ways you can tackle the problem yourself. First try out all your old keys: a box of them, collected over many years, is an advantage. If you cannot find one of the right size and shape, you must assess how much damage you are prepared to risk to the woodwork, as well as how much time and trouble you can spend. The tongue of the lock may be short enough for a drawer to be opened by easing the drawer divider with a jemmy or broad-bladed chisel. Too heavy a hand will, of course, bruise or splinter the surrounding woodwork.

If there is no point in locking the drawer once it has been opened, the tongue can be sawn off by inserting a hacksaw blade between the divider and the drawer itself. Take care not to damage the drawer. It can sometimes be protected by inserting a slip of veneer to prevent the blade from scratching.

Sometimes the screws securing the lock can be reached by removing the drawer above. If there is an obstructing drawer divider you may be able to withdraw this by removing the back of the piece of furniture. The most desperate measure, cutting away part of the drawer divider with a keyhole saw to allow removal of the lock, should only be undertaken *in extremis*.

LOCKS

Keys and locks have a habit of getting separated, especially when furniture changes hands. These days people rarely lock any but the most private drawers and cupboards, but virtually all eighteenth- and nineteenth-century furniture was fitted with locks. New keys can easily be cut for old locks by a competent locksmith, but you will have to take the lock to him. You will find that a single key is usually common to all the drawers in a chest of drawers or bureau, but the desk opening may have a different lock.

To clean neglected locks it is necessary to remove them and, if they are fitted with a shield, to remove this too. Good quality locks are assembled with screws, while cheap ones have the shields riveted on: in these cases the rivet head will have to be filed off. After all the dust and fluff have been removed, soak the lock in paraffin, white spirit or a penetrating oil. If you decide to remove all the springs and wards, lay them out in the order you removed them so that they are easily identified for reassembly. This is only necessary if you are a collector and wish to burnish up all the parts; a gentle rub over with an old toothbrush is normally sufficient for working locks. Dry off the lock and give it a coating of light machine oil before refitting.

MARBLE

Marble is a type of limestone that is easily sawn and carved, and throughout history has been favoured by sculptors and builders. It can be pure white, or varicoloured from the inclusion of mineral salts during its formation.

Marble statuary kept outside should, ideally, have some protection from frost and damp during the winter. This is best done with a wooden 'sentry box' which can be fixed over it and secured against wind without actually touching it. Do not keep marble sculpture outside if you live near the sea: salty air is very damaging. Plants, moss and lichens should not be allowed to grow over statuary, but in removing any be very careful that you do not pull away fragments of the surface or cause further damage.

Whether it is kept outside or indoors, the porous surface of marble makes it susceptible to dirt, dust, pollution or staining, and it can be easily damaged by incorrect cleaning. If in doubt, or if the object in question is very valuable or ancient, take it to a professional stone conservator for advice.

Dust marble with a soft brush with, if necessary, a vacuum cleaner in the other hand. More thorough cleaning should be avoided as much as possible, and detergents, acid-containing cleaning substances or bleaches should never be used.

If you decide you need to wash a piece of marble, first make quite sure it *is* marble and not a look-alike material such as alabaster or painted plaster. Then wipe it with cotton wool swabs damped in a solution of equal parts of white spirit and distilled water with a dash of **non-ionic detergent**, working from the bottom upwards. Rinse with clean swabs damped in distilled water. Alternatively, use Vulpex liquid soap diluted with white spirit (one part of Vulpex to ten or twenty parts of white spirit).

Where more thorough cleaning is required, Bell's 1967 Cleaner or a non-caustic **paint stripper** such as Nitromors can be used: lay it on lightly with a brush and, without leaving it long enough to dry, take it off with swabs dampened in white spirit. Finish the operation by covering the whole piece in a poultice of shredded clean white blotting paper wetted to a pulp in distilled water; leave for several hours until the outside is dry but the inside is still damp and then remove it. Clean off all traces of the blotting paper straight away with cotton wool swabs damped in distilled water.

In certain cases Prelim or Solvol Autosol can be used on marble, but other abrasives should be avoided. After cleaning, protect the surface with **microcrystalline wax** or Bell's marble polish. Another method of whitening and polishing at the same time (useful for white marble only) is to make up a paste with water and french chalk and rub it into the surface until it is dry and burnished. This will also help to conceal deep-seated stains that resist other methods of cleaning.

Marble statuary kept outside can be repaired with quick-drying epoxy resin **adhesive** (Araldite Rapid). Holes can be filled with epoxy resin adhesive mixed with kaolin or titanium oxide, if necessary coloured with powder colours or poster paints. The ready-made **filler** Sylmasta, which can also be tinted, is another option. Indoor pieces should have minor repairs carried out with HMG, Bostik or UHU All Purpose clear adhesives.

MECHANICAL ANTIQUES AND AUTOMATA
As with clocks, the amount of cleaning and renovating you tackle should depend on your own expertise and the value of the object. There is little harm in cleaning the rust off an old sewing machine with paraffin oil or Jenolite, or oiling a typewriter (use a light machine **oil**), but do not tamper with the works of automata (which are nearly always valuable) unless you really know what you are doing. Care for mechanical items in similar ways to CLOCKS, WATCHES and

SCIENTIFIC INSTRUMENTS and treat the different materials they are made from appropriately.

MINIATURES

Miniatures may be painted with oil paint, gouache or watercolour on ivory, vellum, paper or metal. All are delicate and should be treated with great care, kept away from sunlight and out of excessively dry or damp conditions. Dryness will cause cracking and splitting of bases, especially those of ivory, while miniatures on vellum or those painted with watercolour mixed with gum arabic are especially vulnerable to mould growth if allowed to become damp. All miniatures should be protected by glass; most will have their own cases, and these should not be removed. Never clean the frames of miniatures with proprietary metal cleaners or the glasses with commercial glass polishes: many of them contain solvents which can penetrate the frame and damage the miniature painting inside. Dusting or buffing with a chamois leather should be sufficient. If a miniature shows signs of deterioration, do not attempt to restore it yourself but take it to an expert for advice.

MIRRORS

The first mirrors in England were produced during the seventeenth century by a process of blowing long cylinders of molten glass, cutting them open lengthways and then flattening and polishing them. Silvering was done with an amalgam of tinfoil and mercury. Sometimes silver was used, giving a brighter image. The size of the glass sheets that could be produced by the 'sausage' method was limited, so large mirrors of the period were made from several pieces joined together, and the reflection was sometimes distorted.

The silvering on antique mirrors tends to deteriorate, especially in damp conditions, and they may become virtually unusable as looking glasses. At the same time, resilvering can drastically reduce their value and should not be undertaken. Keep mirrors off damp walls and if you have one whose glass has already deteriorated enjoy it simply as decoration.

Clean the glass with a dry linen cloth or chamois leather, taking care not to knock delicate parts of the frame (see also FRAMES). Do not use proprietary cleaners. If the glass is very grubby use a cloth or cotton wool swab dampened in warm soapy water or a little methylated spirit, and then dry with another cloth or chamois; take care not to wet the frame, particularly if it is gilded, nor to let water seep behind the glass. It is a good idea to hold a piece of cardboard against the edge to protect it as you clean.

Periodic checks of hanging supports for mirrors are important: replace ageing cords, wires or chains to avoid potentially catastrophic falls. At the same time inspect the backs of mirrors – usually made of softwood – for woodworm, and treat if necessary.

If you need to replace broken glass in an old mirror, use one of the 'antique' glass ranges. They are darker and less brilliant than standard modern mirror glasses and accord better with old frames.

MOTHER-OF-PEARL

The lustrous, varicoloured interior surface of sea shells has been used for hundreds of years for making or embellishing all kinds of objects, from trinkets and jewellery to boxes and larger items of furniture; it has been used extensively for inlays in wood, lacquer, papier mâché and tortoiseshell. It is a relatively soft material which can be carved and engraved.

A good way to clean mother-of-pearl is to breathe on it and then rub it with your finger. If more thorough measures are necessary, wipe it with cotton wool swabs or a cloth pad damped in soapy water, but do not allow it to get wet; never soak mother-of-pearl, in any form, in water. Prelim or Solvol Autosol can also be used to clean and restore the lustrous surface. Accumulations of dirty wax polish in inlaid mother-of-pearl can be removed very carefully with cotton wool buds damped in white spirit.

Missing fragments of mother-of-pearl veneers or inlays can be replaced by cutting and shaping a new piece with a jeweller's piercing saw or fine-bladed fretsaw and then filing and grinding it to fit. Broken gaming counters are useful stand-bys for such repairs. Use HMG, Bostik or UHU All Purpose clear **adhesives**. For replacing mother-of-pearl cutlery handles see IVORY AND BONE.

MUSICAL BOXES

There are basically two kinds of musical box. One type has a pinned brass cylinder and the other a metal disc with projections: both engage, either directly or (in the disc type) indirectly by means of star wheels, with a tuned steel comb to produce their sounds. Musical boxes vary in size from those that fit into snuff boxes to monster polyphons over six feet tall. The majority of cylinder musical boxes were (and are) made in Switzerland, whereas disc boxes were traditionally made in Germany, particularly in Leipzig.

In caring for musical boxes, similar guidelines apply as for clocks. Keep them free from dust and damp, but do not be tempted to oil the mechanism. Cleaning musical boxes is a complicated business, best left to one of the few experts left in the field (see page 177). The observation of a few important principles will help to ensure the well-being of any musical box. Never stop the mechanism in the middle of a tune, but always let it run to the end; never attempt to take it to pieces without first letting down the spring. Do not play a musical box if the pins on the cylinder or the discs are rusty, corroded or damaged, or if the tune sounds uneven: this is likely to be because the mechanism needs attention and you will do more damage by playing it in poor condition.

When buying a cylinder musical box look carefully at the pins on the cylinder and the tips of the teeth on the comb to make sure they are not bent or broken. Underneath the

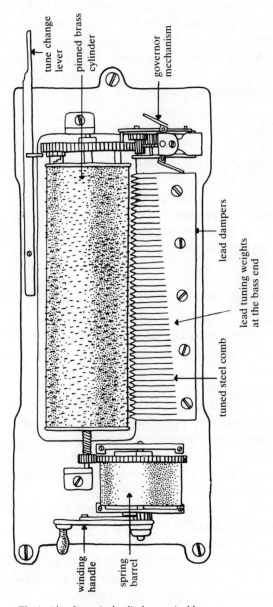

The inside of a typical cylinder musical box

comb, the bass teeth are usually fitted with lead tuning weights and these can be damaged by pollution and become corroded (see LEAD). It is possible to carry out restoration to all these parts but such work is extremely expensive. Replacement of the clockwork parts of the mechanism is easier and therefore less costly.

NICKEL

This bright silver-coloured metal has been used in a variety of ways, from the minting of low-value coins to the plating of tableware. It takes a high polish without tarnishing and was widely used for protective plating before it was superseded by chromium in the twentieth century. It responds to silver cleaners (see SILVER); scratches can be buffed out with a fine **abrasive** such as Solvol Autosol.

NICKEL SILVER

When mixed with copper and zinc, nickel becomes an alloy known as nickel silver, sometimes known as German silver. It is often used as a base for silver-plated items and is marked EPNS (electroplated nickel silver). Treat as silver.

OIL PAINTINGS

Oil paintings are usually executed on canvas stretched on a frame, but they may also be on wood panels of varying timbers, sheets of metal or ivory, or on man-made materials such as hardboard. The resilience, stability, and type of deterioration vary from picture to picture, and cleaning or restoration is a specialist undertaking.

Most oil paintings are not protected by glass. As a result, they are vulnerable to dust, pollution and changes in temperature and humidity. They should therefore not be hung over radiators or fireplaces where they are subject to maximum dirt and dust as well as to convection currents and fluctuations in temperature. Paintings on wood are particularly vulnerable.

Regular inspection of the back as well as the front is vitally important: correcting damage or arresting deterioration at an early stage, if necessary with professional help, will minimize such problems. If you discover woodworm in the stretcher of an oil painting or the wood support of a panel painting it is best to consult an expert rather than treat it yourself: the solvents in proprietary insecticides can seriously damage your painting.

Although most picture conservation techniques are beyond the scope of the amateur, it is helpful to know what a professional restorer does to a painting on canvas. First the old, often discoloured or cracked varnish is removed, revealing the true colouring of the work. Holes, rips and other physical damage are repaired, and missing detail matched in. If the canvas is weak and liable to tear, the picture is removed from its stretcher and lined (or relined) by attaching it to a new canvas either with glue or with hot beeswax. Flaking paint and bubbles are ironed back and, if necessary, the whole work is transferred to a more stable base.

How much of the old varnish or previous restoration should be removed from a painting undergoing conservation is very much a matter of judgement, as is the question of retouching: the techniques involved and the need for sensitive, informed decisions make the conservator's task a challenging one.

If you decide to attempt your own restoration, make sure you are not tampering with a minor masterpiece: take it to a reputable auction house or picture dealer for advice before starting. In any case do not try any but the most conservative procedures.

If the canvas is sagging you may be able to retension it by tightening the wooden wedges at the back: tap them gently with a hammer, in rotation, to keep the tension on the canvas equal in all directions. Alternatively you may need to renail the canvas over its stretcher. Take out the old nails carefully, without splitting the stretcher, and dust the back of the canvas before repositioning it. Use copper or rust-proof nails when reattaching it. Bear in mind that the canvas may be fragile or damaged and can easily split during retensioning; if it seems weak you should probably have it lined.

An oil painting may be cleaned either in a vertical position or flat on a table. In this case the canvas should be supported underneath by slipping acid-free card or pads of tissue between the canvas and the stretcher, to prevent undue pressure during the procedure. When cleaning always work on a small obscure area of the picture first, to make sure you are not causing damage or removing pigment, and that the treatment is working.

To begin with, try removing surface dirt simply with a cotton wool bud or swab damped with spit. Work in circular movements, changing the swab as it becomes dirty; if you find paint as well as dirt on the swab stop at once. In many cases this method will be effective. If not, you can do the same thing with turpentine or white spirit, taking the same care to change the swabs often and to watch for untoward signs.

If your picture is not of any great value and you are determined to clean it more radically you can use Winsor & Newton's Artist's Picture Cleaner: follow the instructions precisely. Any touching up should be done with water-colours. If you need to revarnish your painting, use one of the light retouching spray varnishes, such as that made by Rowney or Rembrandt, which are easy to apply, give good protection and can be removed without difficulty. A light polishing with **microcrystalline wax** can enhance the effect of a successfully cleaned painting.

ONYX

Like agate, onyx is a kind of chalcedony; it is a varicoloured hardstone much used for table tops and ornaments such as table lamps and small boxes. Certain varieties are used for cutting cameos, where the design is cut through the opaque white layer to reveal a more translucent and contrasting colour below. The commonest variety of onyx seen in Europe has a predominantly green colour.

It can be cleaned in warm soapy water and protected with **microcrystalline wax polish**. Repairs should be carried out with HMG, Bostik and UHU All Purpose clear **adhesive**.

ORMOLU

Translated literally from the French, ormolu means 'ground-up gold' and is a term used loosely to describe bronze or other metal castings which have been gilded and applied to furniture, clocks, ceramics and many other objects. The layer of gold is very thin and can be easily damaged by careless handling or over-zealous cleaning. Where it has worn away it should not be touched up or regilded. Damp storage conditions can cause corrosion of the metal base as well as damage to the gilding.

If possible, cleaning should be confined to dusting with a soft brush. Like all kinds of gilded surfaces, ormolu is best not wetted, but stubborn dirt can sometimes be shifted with a cotton bud damped in white spirit or with Vulpex. Ormolu is best protected with a coating of lacquer: the easiest to use is Joy Transparent Paint.

See also **Metal cleaners and polishes**.

PAPER

Works on paper are naturally fragile and most vulnerable to damage by light, damp and acids. They should be kept in clean environments with low light levels and controlled humidity whenever possible, and away from acid substances of all kinds; these include cardboard, fabrics such as felt or velvet, and wood like oak or chestnut, as well as atmospheric pollutants. Acid-free paper and board should always be used for mounting and storage.

Fading of pigments and rotting of paper through exposure to sunlight are irreversible, while mould growths resulting from damp and acid conditions can cause permanent damage. The repair and cleaning of works on paper is a specialized discipline with its own experts, and all valuable prints, maps, watercolours and other pictures in need of restoration should be given professional treatment.

If you attempt your own cleaning, proceed with caution and patience. First, do what you can with dry methods. Dust the picture or document with a soft brush to remove all surface dust; if there are mould growths, brush them off outside. Then clean off smudges and fingermarks with a good quality artist's eraser. Alternatively you can use an erasing powder such as Draft Clean, rubbed on gently with a finger or a soft cloth, working in one direction. Obviously these methods are unsuitable for unfixed chalk or pencil drawings and may be unwise for watercolours except around the edges. A cuttlefish bone can be used as a gentle abrasive to remove spots.

If dry cleaning does not give sufficient improvement you may resort to washing or bleaching: the latter is appropriate for the brown stains or 'foxing' that result from fungal or mildew attack. If there are only a few stains, spot treatment will suffice. Use a mild **bleaching agent** such as chloramine T mixed in a solution of half an ounce of powder to a pint of warm distilled water. Apply the solution to each spot with a soft watercolour brush, and support the paper on a sheet of glass or transparent film to keep it flat while drying.

Washing with plain water is often effective in removing dirt from a print or document. Most printing on paper, whether of pictures or writing, is with oil-bound inks which are fast to water and many solvents. However, watercolours, gouaches, ink, chalk or pastel drawings and works on fugitive coloured papers should not be wetted, and special care should be taken with artists' signatures or inscriptions, which may be in soluble inks. In any case, test a small area of the paper or picture at the outset, to make sure it will not be damaged by wetting.

The print must be supported on a larger sheet of previously wetted glass or transparent flexible film and laid on a flat surface: once wetted, you should not handle the paper itself. Wet the print all over with a sponge and then gently dab the dirty and creased areas; dog-ears can be lifted and flattened out with a fine watercolour brush. Rinse with clean water and then, using a second sheet of supporting glass or plastic (well wetted first), turn the print over and carry out the same process on its other side.

Alternatively, you can immerse the print in a bath of plain tepid water (for about an hour), supporting it, as before, on a wetted sheet of glass or plastic. Use a baking dish, large plastic tray or other flat-bottomed vessel. If the print is very dirty, add a few drops of Synperonic N to the water and leave it for half an hour. If it is seriously foxed, soak it in plain water and then immerse it in a weak solution of bleach (an ounce of chloramine T to a quart of water) and remove it as soon as you see the spots fading and/or the paper lightening.

Whatever washing solution you use, rinse the print for several minutes under gently running water (or in several changes of water in the tray) and then, keeping the print on its support, drain off the excess. Cover the print with layers of clean white blotting paper and then turn it over; remove the support and place more blotting paper over the other side of the print to form a sandwich. Let it dry out under an even weight to keep it flat.

Removing prints or pictures from unsuitable mounts or supports can be tedious and difficult. If in doubt, or if the item is valuable, take it to a professional. When tackling the job at home, observe the principle that the support should be removed from the picture and not the other way round. The easiest to deal with are those that are attached by hinges, but all too many are firmly glued. Sometimes you can slit through the layer of glue with a sharp knife and detach the mount or support; then carefully pare away any remaining glue from the picture with a scalpel.

If you decide that soaking may be the best option (for a print, for example), test the picture or paper for water fastness first. If it seems safe you may be able to soak the picture from the backing in warm water; make sure you remove all the old glue before drying and flattening with blotting paper. Another method is to place the picture face downwards on a clean flat surface and peel the backing off in layers, wetting them as you go.

When reframing a picture use acid-free materials, and starch paste in preference to other adhesives; do not glue the picture to its mount or backing board but attach it with hinges or corners made from acid-free paper or Japanese tissue. The picture should not touch the glass: if you are not using a mount, set a fillet round the inside of the frame. The backing of the frame should be sealed with gummed brown paper tape.

For repairs to paper use Japanese or acid-free tissue paper with a bookbinder's starch paste. It is best to tear, rather than cut, the tissue for a patch to give a softer and less obtrusive edge.

PAPIER MÂCHÉ

Most decorative papier mâché dates from Victorian times, although the process was used in Europe from the seventeenth century onwards, particularly for purposes like coach panels and moulded architectural ornaments. In 1763 one Peter Babel of Long Acre was employing it to manufacture picture frames, and in 1772 Henry Clay of Birmingham patented his 'improved paper ware' which was used most successfully to make trays. A leading producer during the nineteenth century was the firm of Jennens & Bettridge, who took out patents for improvements to the manufacturing and decorating processes, but many other firms, particularly in Birmingham and Wolverhampton, produced small items of furniture and a wide range of decorated wares and boxes throughout the early Victorian period.

As its name suggests, papier mâché is paper pulped with water, glue and various hardening additives, compressed in a mould. It can be sanded down and japanned to a lustrous finish and painted, gilded or inlaid. It is damaged by damp and heat, and is vulnerable to woodworm. Treat this by fumigation rather than liquid treatments which are likely to damage the surface. Vapona strips can be sealed inside a polythene bag with (but not touching) the object and left for several weeks. At the end of the treatment, unseal the bag outside and allow the papier mâché to air for a few hours before bringing it indoors. Thermo Lignum treatment would be a suitable alternative (see **Insecticides**).

Clean papier mâché by dusting carefully to avoid lifting loose fragments of inlaid shell or cracked and flaking areas of the surface. If the finish is in good condition but the surface is dirty, it can be cleaned with swabs of cotton wool damped in soapy water and then rinsed with clean swabs. A final polish with **microcrystalline wax** will give protection and added lustre.

Repairs can be made with HMG, Bostik or UHU All Purpose clear **adhesives**. See MOTHER-OF-PEARL for replacing pearl shell inlays. Chips and missing pieces can be filled with Brummer stopper, coloured with acrylic paint to tone in with surrounding material.

PARCHMENT
Parchment was made from sheep, calf and other animal skins, cured and treated with chalk, smoothed with pumice and sliced to produce sheets suitable for writing. Vellum, from calfskins, is a superior variety of the same thing. During the medieval period, before the development of paper manufacture in the fifteenth century, parchment and

vellum were virtually the only writing or drawing surfaces available in Europe; vellum was mainly used for bookbinding, and as a support for miniature painting. Parchment is particularly susceptible to the depredations of rats and mice, insects and mould; it will distort if allowed to get damp and crack if too dry. Store in acid-free conditions.

Until the beginning of this century parchment continued to be used for legal documents. These were often folded, and if you feel it is essential to flatten them damp the creases at the back over the spout of a steaming kettle, taking care not to get the parchment too wet; then lay it on clean blotting paper with another sheet of blotting paper on top, and flatten it with an even weight. Damaged or very valuable documents should always be taken to an expert for restoration: do not try to repair parchment yourself.

PENWORK
The fashion for painting small items of furniture and all kinds of pale wood boxes in black ink, with or without colours, continued all through the first half of the nineteenth century, and was a favoured pastime among amateur ladies. The designs, usually of neo-classical or chinoiserie subjects, were nearly always 'voided', stencil-fashion, on the black background, and then fine details added. The whole surface was finally varnished. Naturally the tops of penwork tables and boxes are most likely to be worn, scratched or otherwise damaged, and the old varnish may be flaking off. While it is best to leave an object in its original state as far as possible, sometimes the level of disfiguring damage is such that some sort of restoration is called for.

First protect and separate the original surface with a coat of artist's retouching **varnish**, and then use acrylic paints to fill in missing details of the design; apply a final coat of varnish on top. Clean penwork as for FURNITURE *Painted furniture.*

PEWTER

Pewter is an alloy mainly of tin, with copper, antimony and sometimes lead. In France up to eighteen per cent adulteration with lead was permitted and poorer quality antique British pewter also contains lead in varying amounts. The darker the pewter the more lead it is likely to contain. From medieval times the various pewterers' guilds controlled the craft and touchmarks, similar to silver hallmarks, are found on both British and Continental pewter. These marks are not always present, however, and their absence does not detract from a good piece of pewter. Multiple marks may be found, as owners as well as makers impressed them.

Antique pewter is highly collectable and reproductions abound; some are so well made that they are easily mistaken for the genuine article. Take care when buying: look for unworn edges and for touchmarks that are either blurred because they have been cast or too sharp because they have been struck recently.

With age, pewter acquires a deep shadowy patina, provided it is properly cared for and regularly handled. It is soft, however, and can be dented, scratched and bent very easily. Occasionally black wart-like spots appear on the surface: these, like the white powdery corrosion that may affect pewter with a high lead content, should be left alone: consult a metal conservator.

Pewter can be washed in warm soapy water and dried with a cloth. If the surface needs a lift, use a mild **abrasive** such as jeweller's rouge or crocus powder wetted with salad oil, and then wash it in the normal way. Finish with a coating of **microcrystalline wax polish**.

If you have a very dirty and corroded piece, of negligible value, you could clean it by immersing it in paraffin oil for several hours; dry it by wiping it thoroughly with old newspaper and then wash it in warm soapy water, rinse and dry with a clean cloth.

Pushing out dents, and repairs to splits or holes in pewter

should only be undertaken by professional metal conservators.

PHOTOGRAPHS

From a conservation point of view, photographs are among the most fragile of objects. They can be damaged by practically all atmospheric pollutants including those generated by bleaches and ammonia (in household cleaning materials), car exhausts, photocopiers, rubber (including rubber-based adhesives), wood and salt, as well as the usual hazards of light, damp or excessive dryness. Gelatine photographs are especially prone to silverfish, while 35mm cine film made before 1951 may be made from nitrate film which can deteriorate into a brittle condition leading, literally, to spontaneous combustion. Colour negatives and transparencies taken on fast film deteriorate more quickly than those on slow exposures.

Never touch the surface of negatives or photographs, and always keep them in acid-free conditions, preferably in a cool, dark, airy place. Negatives and prints should be stored separately, and glass plates vertically. Photographs of particular value or interest should be rephotographed so that the originals can be handled or displayed as little as possible.

If a photograph becomes wet, do not touch the image, but allow it to dry out naturally, face upwards. Flood-damaged photographs can be stored in a deep freeze (see BOOKS) until professional help is available. If mould appears, do not treat with fungicide: this could cause more damage than it cures. Tears in photographic prints can be repaired from the back with Japanese tissue paper and starch paste. There is very little you can do to renovate damaged or deteriorated photographs yourself, and problems should be referred to a photographic conservator.

PINCHBECK

Pinchbeck, sometimes called poor man's gold, was first produced in the early eighteenth century by Christopher Pinchbeck, a London watchmaker. It is a yellow alloy of five parts copper to one part zinc, with a gilded finish. It was used for watch-cases, snuff boxes and jewellery, and may be distinguished from gold by its lighter weight and the absence of carat marks. It tends to turn dark in time, and the underlying metal has a brassy appearance if the gilding wears through. Clean as for ORMOLU.

PIQUÉ

The inlaying of tortoiseshell, ivory or mother-of-pearl with gold and silver in patterns of tiny studs (*piqué clouté*) or marquetry designs (*piqué posé*) was widely used for small boxes, tea caddies, jewellery and other objects of virtu during the eighteenth and nineteenth centuries.

Dust carefully and preferably with a brush, to avoid lifting any loose or raised inlays. Very dirty or dull surfaces should be cleaned according to the underlying material (see TORTOISESHELL, IVORY or MOTHER-OF-PEARL). Dulled silver inlays can be cleaned with a cotton wool bud damped in Silver Dip and then rinsed with one moistened with water, but try not to touch the base material.

Restoring damaged piqué inlays is a task best left to experts.

PLASTER ORNAMENTS

Before the plastic age, painted plaster models and statues were widely produced as cheap ornaments, and they are now widely collected. Some were finished with hot waxing which penetrated well into the surface to give a marble-like sheen. This was especially favoured for Victorian and Edwardian busts of contemporary personalities and reproductions of classical statues. They are often encrusted with dust, and may look like stone or marble at first sight. If their light weight is not conclusive, a discreet scraping underneath should reveal the soft chalky texture of plaster. More recent plaster figures, such as those given away at fairgrounds, are usually varnished.

Plaster is fragile and easily chipped or rubbed. Waxed examples should be dusted with a brush rather than a duster, to avoid smearing dirt over the waxy surface. Plaster should never be thoroughly wetted, but serious surface dirt and grime can be removed with a swab damped in soapy water; finish by giving the piece another coat of clear wax polish. Repairs can be made with plaster of Paris which can be used both as an adhesive and a filler. Where a larger part has to be restored, use dowels to support the repair inside. Missing parts can be moulded and left to dry for an hour or so. As the plaster is soft in texture it can be finished relatively easily with sandpaper and modelling files.

PLASTICS

These include celluloid, casein, bakelite, PVC, acrylics and epoxy resins, all of which are part of the ever-widening collectors' market. Most become brittle with age and exposure to light, and they are damaged by solvents. Materials like celluloid can cause damage to other substances and should be kept separately from them.

Clean plastics by wiping the surface with swabs damped in soapy water or with a little Solvol Autosol; rinse with clean damp swabs. Do not rub plastics to clean or dry them or you will build up static electricity and they will attract more dust and debris. Repair is sometimes possible with superglue.

RUSHWORK

Chairs have been seated with rushes for many centuries, particularly in parts of the country where materials are locally available, such as the West Midlands. Cleaning is best done by vacuuming or gentle washing: use a cloth dipped in soapy water and wipe in one direction to avoid catching and tearing the rushes. Rinse with clean water and allow to dry thoroughly. Re-rushing a chair is not a difficult job, but the guidance of a specialist or a practical instruction book should be sought at the outset.

SCAGLIOLA

This decorative material, developed in sixteenth- and seventeenth-century Italy to imitate marble and hardstone inlays, is made from coloured marble powders mixed with glue and fixed to a gesso ground under heat. It was used extensively for table tops, ornamental panels and internal architectural features like columns during the eighteenth and nineteenth centuries, and is not always easy to distinguish from true marble. It is, however, softer and will scratch more easily.

Clean scagliola with cotton wool swabs or a cloth damped in warm soapy water, rinse and dry carefully and then polish with **microcrystalline wax**. Minor repairs can be carried out with internal Polyfilla or Brummer stopper.

SCIENTIFIC INSTRUMENTS

Most scientific instruments are made from a combination of materials which must be cared for appropriately (see under the relevant heading). Dust with a soft brush or photographer's puffer brush and keep instruments in clean acid-free conditions. They should be displayed in glass-fronted cabinets, under glass domes or in perspex cases, away from bright light. Wear cotton gloves or cover your hands in acid-free tissue when handling metal items, to protect them from corroding fingermarks. Scientific instruments were given various protective finishes, and these should be carefully preserved whenever possible. Do not use proprietary metal cleaners.

Damage such as corrosion is likely to be the result of deterioration in the lacquer finish. In this case, clean the metal in the appropriate manner (see under separate headings), if necessary removing any remains of old lacquer with Nitromors (yellow tin), and then relacquer the metal with Frigilene or with Joy Transparent Paint. If you need to unscrew parts of the instrument, make sure you use the correct size and type of screwdriver so that you do not damage the screw heads. A finishing coat of **microcrystalline wax polish** is a good idea.

SCREENS

The large folding type of draught screen can present various problems for the repairer. Wooden frames may need renovating, but not the material within the panels, and this will need protection while work is in progress. If possible cover it with polythene sheeting, held in place with masking tape. Leather screens and those decorated with scraps usually have canvas or leather hinges which perish and tear and may have to be replaced.

Most scrap screens have been varnished to protect the paper from wear and tear. If they are very grimy you may be able to revive them by cleaning the dirt off the varnished surface with cotton wool swabs damped in soapy water. Restick any lifting scraps with wallpaper paste or PVA bookbinding paste, and repair torn or damaged areas with other scraps of an appropriate type. Reproduction Victorian and Edwardian scraps are easy to find if you do not have a supply of old ones; or you can cut up old postcards or other pictures to fit the subject matter and style of the screen. You can 'antique' them with a slightly tinted clear **varnish** that tones in with the rest of the screen.

SCREWS

Screws that have become embedded can cause much delay and irritation. First try a drop or two of paraffin. If this is not successful, Plus Gas or WD40 may work. Where screws have become rusted into wood or metal try heating the heads with the red-hot tang of a file or other suitable iron. The heat first makes the screw expand and the subsequent cooling causes it to contract and, with luck, frees it.

With really obstinate screws it is worth grinding down an old screwdriver to the exact size of the slot in the screw head to get the maximum purchase without tearing the screw head. A burred screw becomes progressively more difficult to turn. Place your screwdriver in the slot of the screw and strike it smartly with a mallet; work it clockwise and anti-clockwise. The pressure on the screwdriver can be increased by securing an adjustable spanner at the top end of the screwdriver blade and using it as an extra lever while holding the screwdriver down in the screw head with the other hand.

As a last resort you may have to drill out the screw completely, using a high speed metal drill. First use a centre punch to dent the screw head; this makes drilling possible. The resulting hole can usually be concealed to an acceptable extent by fitting a wooden plug of a similar variety of timber.

SHAGREEN
Greenish shark-skin or fish-skin, sometimes flattened to produce a granular appearance, has been used for covering boxes of all kinds, small decorative items, scientific instruments and sword hilts since the eighteenth century. It can be cleaned with swabs damped in warm soapy water and polished with **microcrystalline wax.**

SHEFFIELD PLATE AND SILVER PLATE
Sheffield plate was produced from the mid-eighteenth century to the mid-nineteenth by fusing a small piece (or billet) of silver on to a large billet of copper and rolling it out until the layer of silver was extremely thin. The bonded metals could then be fashioned into tea services, candlesticks and many other domestic objects. By this technique the edges of

the sheets were not silver-plated and were usually 'lapped' with silver wire to protect them from wear. The backs of the sheets were normally left unplated, and the insides of vessels such as tea urns or tureens were tinned. The copper base will show through worn Sheffield plate but it should not be replated.

Sheffield plate was superseded by electroplating, in which a prefabricated metal object is coated with an electrically transferred deposit of silver. Electroplating was found to be most successful on nickel silver or Britannia metal (q.v.) and examples are marked EPNS or EPBM. They can be replaced if necessary.

Both types of silver plate tarnish easily, especially if they are exposed to atmospheric pollutants, smoke from fires or acid-producing materials such as wool, felt or velvet. They should be displayed in cabinets (but not those made of oak) or stored in cupboards wrapped in acid-free tissue or Tarn-prufe bags; keep silver and plated wares away from news-paper or rubber bands.

Clean plated wares as rarely as possible: any polishing, no matter how carefully done, will remove a little of the silver from the surface. The gentlest method is to wash the piece in warm soapy water, rinse and dry thoroughly and then polish with a Long Term Silver Cloth. Tarnished items can be cleaned with Silver Dip, while long-term silver polishes are good for general care and reduce the need for frequent cleaning.

Silver plate can be protected with a lacquer such as Frigilene: in this case do not use long-term polishes first, but prepare the surface with a silver cleaner such as Silvo or Silverglit and then wash well in soapy water to remove any traces of polish, dust or grease. A well-applied coating of lacquer will give protection from tarnish for several years, but it will eventually need to be removed (with acetone) and replaced.

Greenish deposits on old Sheffield plate can be due to

verdigris and may be successfully cleaned off with methylated spirit applied with a swab. Repairs should be carried out by a professional (see also SILVER).

SHELLS AND SHELLWORK

Loose shells can be washed in warm soapy water, rinsed and dried carefully, but decorative shellwork in which adhesives are used should only be wiped with dampened swabs. Dust can be a problem with elaborate pieces and they should always be kept under domes or in glass cases. If you need to replace broken or detached shells use UHU or Bostik All Purpose clear **adhesives.**

SILVER

Most antique silver should be easy to recognize and to date by its hallmarks; the English assaying system, in operation since 1300, is probably the oldest form of consumer protection, and other countries have similar ways of assessing and identifying precious metals. Without reliable hallmarks, or if a fake is suspected, the genuineness and purity of silver can only be determined by testing with nitric acid. Make a small scratch deep enough to penetrate plating, and expose the underlying metal. A drop of acid (or a mark from a nitric acid pencil) on the scratch will react light grey to sterling silver; a dark grey reaction indicates sub-sterling silver, while most base metals give a greenish, fizzy reaction. After testing, wash the object in running water.

Silver is easily tarnished by sulphur compounds occurring in the atmosphere through all kinds of pollution and in certain substances such as rubber, household paints and textiles like wool, felt and velvet. Store as for SILVER PLATE. Silver cutlery especially is tarnished by vinegar, salt, egg, brussels sprouts and even normal water supplies which are chlorinated; it should always be washed as soon as possible after use and dried thoroughly. Fingermarks can accelerate the process of tarnishing, which is why most silver should be handled as little as possible, and preferably with cotton gloves on. It is soft and easily dented or scratched, and over-conscientious polishing will wear away surface decoration and cause holes in embossed work.

Keeping silver in acid-free or at least acid-reduced conditions and handling it carefully will reduce the need for cleaning and polishing: this should be done as rarely as possible as each time the surface is cleaned a minute layer of silver is removed with the tarnish. Clean dust and dirt by washing the silver in warm soapy water and then rinse and dry it thoroughly; buff with a Long Term Silver Cloth or with Hagerty silver gloves.

Tarnished pieces are best cleaned with Silver Dip or the mildly abrasive Silver Foam. If you are cleaning silver by immersing it in Silver Dip, it is best to use just enough, in a separate jar, and then throw it away; stale and reused Silver Dip can be damaging. Alternatively, wet a swab with Silver Dip and wipe it over the surface of the silver; tarnish can be removed from the crevices of decoration with a cotton bud wetted with Silver Dip. After cleaning silver with any of these preparations, wash it in warm soapy water and rinse before drying.

If you feel that polishing is essential, use Long Term Silver Polish rather than proprietary silver cleaners without tarnish inhibitors. You should not resort to plate powders, which are abrasive as well as messy to use, unless you need to rub out a scratch. While polishing, hold the piece by its body and not by the handle, base or other vulnerable part. It is most important to support it in your hand or on your lap. Never work on a table or other hard surface where you have less control over the pressure you exert, and are likely to cause damage. Supporting each part of the item as you go, polish in circles; wipe off the polish with a soft cloth, taking care to remove all traces from the crevices of decorated pieces, if necessary with a soft toothbrush.

Wooden handles, for example on teapots, should be given

a coat of wax polish to keep them in good condition. If repairs are needed, they should be undertaken by a professional craftsman through a silversmith or jeweller. The insides of teapots can be cleaned periodically by filling them with warm water and a dessertspoonful of soda crystals; leave overnight and then rinse away. Neither wooden nor ivory handles should be immersed in water.

Verdigris or spots of tarnish that resist other cleaners can be removed by dabs of methylated spirit (as for SILVER PLATE) or ammonia applied on a cotton wool swab (in a cool airy place). Do not use ammonia on plated pieces as it can damage copper. The surface of silver treated with ammonia may be slightly rough; rub it with plate powder and it will gradually improve.

Do not use Silver Dip or abrasives on silver decorated with the blackened patterns known as niello: you will destroy them. Clean very gently with Long Term Silver Polish.

Like plated wares, ornamental silver can be protected with a lacquer such as Frigilene (see SHEFFIELD PLATE AND SILVER PLATE).

STAMPS

Ever since their introduction, both 'mint' and used stamps have been popular collectors' items. The more perfect the example, the higher its value, with certain types carrying a premium. These include stamps attached to selvages which bear printers' register and colour guides or sheet numbers, and 'gutters' or sheets of stamps with an unprinted area down the middle. Stamp collectors look for used examples in undamaged condition, with good clean strikes of the franking stamp, or unused ones in perfect state and unmounted; any stamp which has a mistake in the printing will assume additional value. For all kinds of reasons stamped envelopes or 'covers' may be particularly valuable: if in doubt, do not detach the stamps from an envelope.

As with any collecting field, stamps have been subject to deceptive practices and fakery, and the 'investing' collector should be wary of the risks and pitfalls.

There is nothing to be done to clean or restore stamps, other than to soak used examples off envelopes in a tray of lukewarm water; allow them to dry, gum side up, on sheets of clean blotting paper and then press under a heavy book.

STONEWORK

All outside stonework, whether of hard materials such as granite and slate or the softer limestones, is vulnerable to damage from acid rain, frost, corroding metals and plants such as moss, lichen and ivy. Whenever possible, statues should be placed on plinths with damp-proof membranes to prevent rising damp and salts from the ground penetrating the stone. If they need to be supported or secured, stainless steel should be used in preference to other metals. However picturesque, plant growths are damaging and should be carefully removed. For protection from frost see MARBLE.

Any signs of deterioration in the surface of stonework should be a signal to leave it well alone and consult a professional conservator. However, stonework in sound condition can be cleaned periodically by spraying with a hose and, once the dirt has been loosened, brushing it off with a soft brush. If necessary use a **fungicide** such as dichlorophen to clear algae, mildew and lichen. Bell's 1967 Cleaner, or Vulpex diluted with water (one part of Vulpex to six or seven parts of cold tap water), can be used for cleaning slate, stone and bricks. Repair as for MARBLE.

STRAW-WORK

Objects covered in straw marquetry are obviously fragile and should be kept away from bright light, heat or damp conditions. Dust with a brush rather than a duster, to avoid catching the delicate surface. With patience and dexterity, missing fragments of straw can be matched and replaced, using a starch or PVA paste.

TAXIDERMY

Preserved natural history specimens are particularly vulnerable to the ravages of insects and vermin as well as the usual problems of dirt, damp and pollution. They should be kept in glass cases whenever possible, and inspected regularly for infestation. Concealed mothballs or paradichlorobenzene crystals inside cases can provide long-term protection.

Dust stuffed animals, birds and fish gently with a soft brush or photographer's puffer brush, taking especial care with feathers as these can easily be detached. For very large dusty specimens hold a vacuum cleaner with a covered nozzle in your other hand to remove the dust while you brush, but do not vacuum the specimen itself. Always brush in the same direction as the fur or feathers lie. For dry cleaning, fuller's earth, dusted over the fur or feathers, left for a few minutes and then brushed off, can shift more tenacious dirt. Rearrange the fir with a comb and then stroke gently with your hand. Feathers can be resettled with a needle.

Clean hard parts like antlers, teeth, hooves and eyes with cotton wool swabs damped in isopropyl alcohol. If fur or feathers are falling out, skins are disintegrating, or holes appear in legs, feet or beaks, or if you find insect remains or droppings in or around the specimen, you should suspect attack from mites, moth, booklice or carpet beetle and take action. An insecticide such as Vapona can be effective, but you may need to fumigate (see **Insecticides**). If you are in doubt about the cause of any deterioration, consult a taxidermist.

While it is wise not to tamper with the skins of specimens apart from cleaning them, you may need to touch up such areas as beaks, noses, paws or the insides of mouths and ears. Only use reversible **adhesives** like HMG, Bostik or

UHU All Purpose. Wax can be used for filling. If you must recolour any parts use acrylic paints as they are easy to mix and match, and are quick-drying. Apply a coat of clear **varnish** where a glossy finish is needed.

The refurbishing of the case is sometimes as important as the care of the specimen itself. Try to preserve its antique look, while making sure it provides adequately sealed protection for the object inside it. You can reinforce background settings with dried grasses and other plants, pebbles and so forth (always make sure they are really dry). Use an epoxy putty or a plaster **filler** to represent the ground or to support plants; set them in, arrange pebbles and sprinkle sand before it dries and then paint (with acrylic paints) if necessary.

If you need to replace a pane of glass in a case or make a completely new one, get the glass cut to your precise measurements by a builder's merchant and fix the sheets together with brown paper tape or Tuftape.

TEA CADDIES

Tea was an expensive luxury during the late seventeenth and eighteenth centuries and containers to hold it were appropriately grand; they were usually lockable and designed, like the rest of the tea equipage, for ostentatious display. The larger boxes, often fitted with canisters of precious metals, enamel or porcelain, were known as tea chests until the late eighteenth century when the word caddy came into use. This is a corruption of the Malay word *kati*, denoting a measure of weight of just over one pound. Tea chests, canisters and caddies are to be found in all kinds of materials and decorated with a variety of techniques: they should be cared for according to the materials and decorative processes with which they were made.

The interior of the typical wooden tea caddy is divided into compartments to hold green (unfermented) and black (fermented) tea, sometimes with a central glass bowl for sugar. The tea compartments were nearly always lined with tin or lead foil and this should be preserved, even if torn or damaged. Never attempt relining.

TEAPOTS

Tannic acid in tea causes staining in teapots of all materials and in extreme cases the stain can penetrate china and discolour the outside of the pot. Teapots in general use therefore require regular cleaning, while those for display may need to be cleaned when you first acquire them. Fill the pot with warm water and dissolve a tablespoon of borax or Steradent in it. Leave it to stand for several hours before wiping out the inside with a nylon washing-up scourer; use a wire-handled bottle brush for the spout. Obviously this treatment should be modified for very precious teapots, which should be wiped with a cloth rather than a scourer or brush. For an alternative treatment with soda crystals, see SILVER.

TERRACOTTA

Terracotta is baked red clay, and it has been used for thousands of years to make tiles, bricks, architectural decoration, statues and pots for use both inside and outside. It can be left in its natural porous state, or painted, glazed or burnished. Outside, it is particularly susceptible to damage from frost. For care and repair, see STONE and CERAMICS.

TEXTILES

Of all materials, textiles are among the most destructible: wear and tear, dirt and dust, light and heat, damp and insects, pollution and careless handling all contribute to deterioration and disintegration. Even the substances with which they were made, like certain dyes or finishes, are sometimes inherently destructive. While detailed procedures of care and repair should be studied in specialist books or carried out by professionals, certain guidelines for conservation should be followed by anyone dealing with old textiles of any description.

Light is most damaging and fading irreversible, so textiles should always be stored in a dark place and, if displayed at all, hung on walls which the sun or bright lights do not reach; curtains or blinds should be used to darken rooms which are not in use. Never use spotlights on textiles. Because they absorb moisture which will cause rot and encourage fungal attack, textiles must be protected from dampness or excessive humidity.

Textiles should be kept in acid-free conditions and in ways that minimize stresses to the fibres. Use acid-free tissue for wrapping and padding, and whenever possible avoid folding. Instead, roll them, right side out, over tubes. The larger and heavier the textile, the wider the tube should be. If you use a cardboard or plastic tube, cover it with acid-free tissue first. Secure them with tapes rather than elastic bands or string.

Cotton or linen bags and covers should be used for storage in preference to polythene which can cause static electricity and attract dust as well as sealing in moisture. Well-washed old cotton shirts can be invaluable for this.

Pins, especially rusty ones, should be removed and paper labels or other attachments put into envelopes and sewn on. Costumes should be hung on padded hangers, and items unsuitable for rolling should be padded with tissue. Textiles that have to be folded should be interleaved with acid-free tissue.

Mothballs or Vapona strips can be useful in preventing moth attack, but they should not come into direct contact with textiles. Certain herbs – mint, rosemary, lavender, southernwood, thyme and santolina among them – also repel moths. Silica gel crystals can help to combat moisture but must be monitored.

Dirt is most damaging of all, and it is not always possible to wash or dry clean delicate fabrics. One of the safest methods of removing dust and loose dirt is with a vacuum cleaner, but make sure it does not suck too vigorously. If you are vacuuming fine fabrics, cover the nozzle with a piece of net or old nylon stocking; take special care not to suck up loose or damaged threads. Fragile items can be laid flat and covered with a larger piece of nylon gauze, pinned down, and then vacuumed. For large items, use an embroiderer's ring frame fitted with gauze, and move it across the surface of the textile, vacuuming through it as you go.

Alternatively, place the embroidery or other textile face down on a piece of clean tissue paper and tamp it gently with your fingers; carefully sweep dust particles out of the crevices of the stitchery with a fine soft brush. A little kaolin brushed over the surface and left for a few minutes before vacuuming or tamping can also be effective. Remove fluff and similar debris from the pile of materials like velvet, felt and velour with sticky tape (but do not use this method on rotting or very precious fabrics).

A more radical dry cleaning method, for small items, is with bicarbonate of soda. Sprinkle bicarbonate of soda all over the bottom of a box or tray (a plastic photographer's tray is ideal), lay the embroidery or other textile down and then sprinkle again with bicarbonate of soda. Leave for several days before removing all traces of the powder by the tamping method or by vacuuming.

Robust old textiles may be successfully dry cleaned, especially if they are dirty from grease or oils rather than water-based soiling (best removed by washing). Some dry-cleaning firms make a speciality of antique textiles, but if you cannot find one of these in your district, protect each piece by tacking it between old nylon net curtains or into a nylon net bag and clean it in a coin-operated dry-cleaning machine. Do one item at a time to prevent damage from weight and friction. Valuable or historic items should always be taken to a professional conservator for cleaning.

Somewhere between dry cleaning and washing is the

foam-cleaning method, which is more suitable for delicate textiles than immersing. Lay the textile face upwards on a plastic or acetate surface and dab it with the foam from a well-lathered lukewarm solution of Dreft, Woolite or Stergene (with your fingers): the dirt should fall through on to the back. Rinse by sponging with softened lukewarm water and allow to dry. If at any time colour appears on your hands or the sponge stop at once and dry the piece with a hairdrier (which should be on hand throughout the procedure).

Washing may be the best course for textiles such as lace and whitework embroidery, linen or cotton baby clothes, underwear, napery and bed-linens. If you are thinking of washing coloured items such as samplers or upholstery fabrics, make quite sure the colours are fast before immersing. Apply wet cotton wool to all the colours on an unobtrusive part of the piece (preferably on the back): if any colour appears on the cotton wool, you should avoid washing. Always remove linings and wash them separately. Silks and materials with metal threads or embellishments should not be washed, nor should tapestries, painted fabrics, flags or banners.

Lissapol, Vulpex, Synperonic N, Stergene, Dreft, Woolite or Saponaria can be used, but not other commercial detergents or biological washing powders. Do not use bleaches or starches, and always use lukewarm, soft water; if necessary soften it with Calgon. Protect fragile items by tacking them on to nylon net curtains or supporting them with a sheet of acetate film while they are wet. Do not rub or squeeze, but gently press with a sponge and change the water as it gets dirty. Rinse thoroughly, and finally with distilled water.

Allow textiles to dry naturally and preferably flat, away from bright light or artificial heat. They can be smoothed or even pinned into shape (use stainless steel or brass lace pins on a board protected with polythene). Thick or coloured items can be pressed between layers of towelling or blotting paper before being laid out to dry. Ironing, if it is necessary at all, should be kept to a minimum and done on a cool setting on the back of the material. Steaming (not too hot and not too wet) can be an effective way of removing creases in delicate fabrics, and is the best way to revive tired velvet.

Stubborn stains are best left alone: proprietary cleaners are likely to do more damage. If you are tempted to bleach out a mark, use a very weak solution of hydrogen peroxide and soak the material for no more than ten minutes; rinse thoroughly and then allow to dry as above. Do not attempt to whiten old lace: it was usually intended to be a creamy colour and bleaching will weaken the fibres.

In repairing textiles, always sew and never glue them. Make sure you sew between threads rather than through them and thus causing them to split and be further weakened. Fragile damaged pieces, such as silk embroideries, can be supported on nylon net, or even sandwiched between two layers. Use a man-made thread with tacking or couching stitches.

An embroidery or other textile that is to be framed should be fastened to a backing sheet of acid-free card or hardboard covered with linen or cotton. This should be slightly larger than the textile. A backing material, or tapes sewn along the edges of the embroidery, may provide extra support and prevent undue stress to the textile itself.

Always use a fillet or mount to prevent a framed textile from touching the glass. Seal the back with brown paper tape to prevent insects and dust from getting inside the frame. Obviously embroideries in old frames with ill-fitting glass or backs which are not dust-proof should be taken out and inspected, cleaned if necessary, and replaced with acid-free materials and correct framing (see also UPHOLSTERY and WALL HANGINGS).

TINWARE

Tin plating over other metals, most often iron, was widely used on kitchenware and for lining food containers because it does not rust and therefore protects other metals from deterioration and from tainting preserved foodstuffs. It was only superseded relatively recently when plastic and lacquer coatings were introduced into the canning industry. High quality copper saucepans are still coated with tin on the interior surfaces.

Antique household items made from tin plate are often in need of renovation. Typically, the coating of bright tin will have worn away in places and the duller steel body may have started to rust. The problem is to remove the rust and shine up the steel without destroying the remaining tin coating.

First wash the object in hot water containing a little washing soda. Clean rusted edges and bare patches carefully with a fine **abrasive**, taking care to preserve the remaining coating of tin as far as possible. Jenolite Jelly can be used to remove spots of rust. As moisture can penetrate folds and cracks where the tinsmith has made joins, place the object in a warm oven for a few minutes to make sure it is thoroughly dry and then polish with **microcrystalline wax**.

Japanned tin plate or *tôle* was used during the eighteenth and nineteenth centuries for colourful decorative items such as trays, candlesticks, boxes and vessels. From the late nineteenth century onwards painted tin plate was used widely for toys and for containers such as money boxes, biscuit tins and other packaging.

Like utilitarian tinware, japanned and painted tin can usually be washed (but not soaked) in soapy water and dried carefully. If it is still dirty, clean the surface with a swab damped in methylated spirit, but stop at once if the paint appears to be fugitive. Do not wash tin toys, but try the spirit treatment. Rust can be removed by carefully scraping it off the surface and then applying **rust remover** (Renaissance De-corroder, Jenolite or Modalene) on cotton wool buds, avoiding the paintwork. If the painted surface is in good condition it should be protected with **microcrystalline wax polish**. Scratched or damaged paintwork can be touched up with acrylic paints and waxed once the paint has hardened, but repainting should be avoided.

Repairs can be carried out (from the back of the object if possible) by soldering with lead and a non-corrosive flux or mending with an epoxy resin **adhesive**.

TOOLS
Old woodworking and all kinds of other tools are much sought after, not just by collectors or for decoration, but by those who work with them in traditional crafts. Using them correctly and with skill is the best way to maintain them. Tools which are not in use should be cared for in the appropriate manner for individual materials (see IRON AND STEEL and FURNITURE).

TORTOISESHELL
Before the advent of plastics the shell of the hawksbill turtle was used to manufacture a multitude of small objects from boxes to combs. When heated it can be manipulated into a variety of shapes or press-moulded to form decoration in relief. As it is naturally translucent, it was often stained with various coloured dyes or mounted on coloured backgrounds to enhance the natural beauty of its figuring. Tortoiseshell will turn milky grey if it is exposed to strong sunlight, and this condition is irreversible.

Clean tortoiseshell with cotton wool swabs dipped in soapy water and rinse with clean damp swabs; do not allow the surface to get very wet. If it is grimy, it can be cleaned with a mild **abrasive** such as Prelim or Solvol Autosol. A little olive oil or almond oil rubbed into the surface on your fingers can give lustre; **microcrystalline wax polish** is similarly effective.

You can replace broken or loose fragments of tortoiseshell with animal glue or PVA; for filling see BOULLE and PIQUÉ.

TREEN

Turnery and other ornamental wood wares should be cared for as FURNITURE and protected with **microcrystalline wax polish.**

TUNBRIDGE WARE

Turned wood souvenirs known as Tunbridge wares were being produced in London and the Tonbridge area of Kent by the seventeenth century and various forms of treen were a speciality of Tunbridge Wells throughout the eighteenth century. During the Regency period they included painted and printed wares, but early in the nineteenth a distinctive type of mosaic ware was developed by several local manufacturers who used mainly native woods. The later nineteenth-century Tunbridge output consists almost entirely of boxes and small items such as needlework tools and desk accessories in stickware or micro-mosaic. The technique involves the building up of pictures and designs using lengths of variously toned woods in square sections of about one millimetre. These were glued together and then sliced thinly to form veneers.

Tunbridge ware should be kept in similar conditions as furniture, and not exposed to extremes of temperature or humidity. Dust mosaic wares carefully to avoid catching loose fragments which may be lifting from the surface, and polish with **microcrystalline wax.**

Most Tunbridge wares were coated in varnish which has often deteriorated. If possible this should be left alone, or merely cleaned with swabs damped in soapy water, but if it obscures the design you may need to replace it. A **paint stripper** (Nitromors) brushed on and then removed with very fine wire wool may be successful, but take great care not to lift mosaic patterns. Clean off with white spirit on cotton wool swabs and then sand down with a fine garnet paper before revarnishing: apply several coats of artist's retouching **varnish.**

While damage to veneers may be repaired in the usual way (see FURNITURE), fragments of micro-mosaic may have to be patched with a **filler** such as Brummer stopper or with hard waxes of suitable colours. If a large area is missing, you may be able to make a cosmetic repair by applying a section of light-coloured veneer and then colouring it with acrylics or coloured inks to match the design. The varnish will alter the colour, so test a separate piece to make sure that the colour balance is accurate.

UPHOLSTERY

The reupholstering of antique furniture is a wide subject which cannot be covered in this book, but a few points of principle can be made. Like all textiles, upholstery must be kept clean, dry and protected from strong light. Regular vacuuming is the best way to remove dust and surface dirt: cover the nozzle of the vacuum cleaner with net. The best way to preserve antique upholstery on chairs is with case covers which can be removed for special occasions, or with loose covers.

If you need to reupholster, try to preserve as much of the original material as possible, and at least make sure the new upholstery is carried out in an appropriate style and material: if necessary, consult a good reference book on period interiors and upholstery.

Small repairs, undertaken sooner rather than later, can postpone the need for more radical renovation. Among these, the replacement of buttons on deep-buttoned upholstery is a relatively simple task. Remove the back covering of the upholstery and work from behind, using a special long needle with a point at both ends and upholstery twine, anchored with a pad of hessian or similar material (see diagram on page 142).

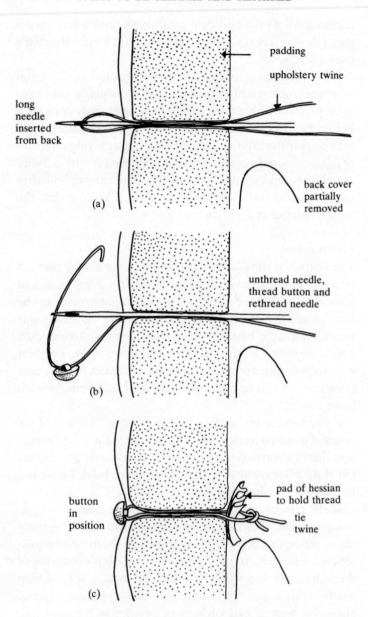

Renewing a button on deep-buttoned upholstery

The replacement of gimps and trimmings may also be undertaken. They should be sewn on with a curved needle. See also TEXTILES.

WALL HANGINGS

When tapestries and other fabrics are hung, it is important that they are not strained or stretched. Most should be attached by the top edge and hung an inch or so away from the wall to allow circulation of air and to protect them from possible damp. They should never be hung in bright light or above radiators and they should be lined to protect the backs from dust.

The best method of suspension is Velcro, which allows the weight to be distributed evenly along the top edge. Sew the fluffy side of the Velcro through both the lining and the textile along the top edge, and fix the prickly side to a batten on the wall with tacks along the top. If you use rings and hooks, make sure they are no more than eight inches apart, even when tape is used to reinforce the top edge of the hanging.

Inspect hangings regularly for moth and other insects, and vacuum from time to time to keep them clean (see TEXTILES).

WATCHES

Because they are carried about, watches are regulated by a balance wheel and balance spring (or hair spring) rather than a pendulum. They should be wound regularly and never over-wound; even when a watch is not in use it should be wound from time to time to exercise the movement. Set the hands by turning them clockwise rather than backwards. Most watches have a regulating screw or lever at the back with a plus or minus sign for making the watch go faster or slower. If you have difficulty in adjusting the timing in this way, take the watch to a professional repairer. Watch movements should be professionally cleaned and overhauled every few years. Clean the outside as little as possible: if it is silver, use a Long Term Silver Cloth from time to time, but never powder, polish or water. To prevent fingermarks (and deposits of acid from the skin) wear cotton gloves when handling a collection of watches.

WAX ARTEFACTS

The basis of most antique wax objects is beeswax, often mixed with other materials such as tallow, chalk, resin, hard vegetable waxes and, for the last century or so, paraffin wax. In ancient Egypt, wax models were placed in the tombs of the Pharaohs; from the Middle Ages onwards wax was cast to form official seals, and more recently it has been used to make artificial flowers and fruit, dolls' heads (see DOLLS), three-dimensional pictures and portraits, and models of all kinds.

Wax is obviously most vulnerable to heat, but it is easily cracked, chipped or broken, and is made more brittle by age and cold; colours can fade, while artefacts like flowers and fruit or portraits can literally absorb dust and dirt if not protected under glass domes or in sealed frames.

Dust wax objects gently with a soft brush or with a photographer's puffer brush, and clean more tenacious dirt with cool soapy water applied with an artist's brush. The colour of many wax models is contained in the thin outer coating, so be careful not to wash it away. Do not attempt to clean precious or exceptionally dirty items yourself: repairs are also best left to an expert.

ZINC AND SPELTER

Zinc is used for galvanizing iron to prevent it rusting and, alloyed with lead, to make spelter. This was cast into decorative objects and statues in imitation of bronze during the nineteenth century. It is distinguishable from bronze by its lighter weight, greyish colour and softer, more brittle nature. It was often painted.

To clean it, dust with a soft brush or wipe carefully with cotton wool wetted in soapy water (first making sure that the paint will not be damaged) and then rinse and dry thoroughly. Spelter sculpture that is kept outside should be washed periodically with soapy water, thoroughly rinsed and, when it is completely dry, protected with **microcrystalline wax**. If it shows any sign of deterioration it should be brought indoors at once and advice sought from a metal conservator. Repairs to spelter can be made with Araldite.

Section Two
Materials, Equipment and Techniques

Abrasives

An abrasive is a substance for scratching, grinding and wearing down by rubbing. The coarser and harder the abrasive, the quicker the wearing-down process and the deeper the scratches. The finer the abrasive, the finer the finish. Indeed it is difficult to determine when abrasion stops and polishing begins: polishing is a mild form of abrasion. Abrasives come in many forms: hard, sharp particles adhered to paper, incorporated into greasy bars or suspended in liquids, incorporated into blocks or crushed into powders. They may also be formulated with corrosives and/or solvents for specific purposes.

Wire wool/steel wool is one of the most useful and versatile of abrasive materials, acting both as scourer and burnisher. It is sold in various grades, the finest being 0000. It can be used for both wood and metal finishing, either dry or with a lubricant such as white spirit, machine oil or a polish.

Solvol Autosol is a mildly abrasive cream, designed for cleaning chromium, but useful for cleaning and polishing many other materials, including brass and copper, marble and tortoiseshell.

Prelim is a specially formulated non-scratch cleaning paste, used in the professional restoration of metals, enamel and ceramic surfaces.

147

Most abrasives are available from ironmongers. Less commonly used grades of wire wool and abrasive papers are available from specialist suppliers like Myland*, Fiddes* or Wastnage*, and abrasive powders from Walsh*; Solvol Autosol is available from car and bicycle spares shops. Prelim is available from Picreator Enterprises* or Conservation Resources*.

Abrasive papers

Sandpaper, sold in several grades of coarseness, is still widely used, but some of the others do not wear out so quickly.

Carborundum paper, emery paper and *wet and dry paper* are all varieties of paper or cloths coated with dark grey abrasive and are specifically used by the engineering and coach-building trades for rubbing down metal and cellulose painted surfaces. They are used for smoothing and polishing all kinds of metals. Wet and dry is used for rubbing down fillers.

Garnet paper, sold in several grades of coarseness, is useful for smoothing and finishing all kinds of wood. Work from a fairly coarse grade for initial smoothing, to fine for finishing.

Jeweller's emery paper is an abrasive used for metals, finer than engineering grades. The finest will produce a high polish on iron and steel.

Lubrasil is a silicone-lubricated paper, used in french polishing, that remains unclogged much longer than other varieties.

Micromesh abrasive smoothing paper (from Hobby Aids*) is fine enough to polish Perspex, and is most useful in ceramic restoration.

Abrasive powders

Grinding and polishing powders, of varying fineness, are mainly but not exclusively used for metal finishing. The principal ones are *carborundum powder, crocus powder, emery powder, jeweller's rouge, pumice, rottenstone, tripoli powder* and *whiting*.

Acrylic sheet
Marketed in many different forms, this hard but scratchable plastic material can be used instead of glass in some circumstances. It is available from DIY shops and artists' suppliers.

Acrylic film or acetate is transparent and flexible, providing a non-stick surface for repair jobs. It is available from artists' suppliers.

Adhesives
No adhesive is suitable for every job, so make sure you use an appropriate one, and follow the manufacturer's instructions, bearing in mind that these will always tell you what the glue *will* stick but rarely what it will not. Use reversible adhesives whenever possible. Gluing is easy, provided you follow a few simple rules and do not try to take short cuts.

1. You cannot stick fresh air together. Surfaces to be joined must come into close contact with each other. Filling up a slack joint with extra glue will not make a durable repair. Maximum surface contact is essential for the join to be successful.

2. You cannot stick together dust, dirt, grease or perished glue. Previous repairs must be separated and cleaned thoroughly. Old glue can be scraped out or scrubbed away with warm water, acetone or other solvent depending on the type of glue; grease can be removed with suitable solvents which must be left to dry out thoroughly. Make sure the surfaces are completely dry before applying new adhesive.

3. Apply the glue to both surfaces unless otherwise instructed.

4. Once glued together, the joint should be held firmly and not disturbed until the glue has had time to set thoroughly. Drying time will vary with different adhesives, but with

non-quick-drying types such as animal glue, joints should be left under pressure for at least twelve hours. Hardening time is also affected by temperature: the higher, the quicker. You can devise all kinds of ingenious methods of cramping, but you should prepare your method before applying the glue. Clothes pegs, elastic bands, self-adhesive tape, heavy weights and elastic material (like strands cut from old inner tubes of tyres) wound several times round the work are among the many possibilities.

5. Always remove excess glue as soon as possible.

Acrylic adhesives
These clear liquid glues are suitable for a wide variety of sticking jobs and are reversible with acetone. Their setting time ranges from ten seconds to twenty minutes and can be speeded up by applying heat. They are applied direct from the tube in a thin layer to both surfaces to be joined. If the material is porous, apply two coats before bringing the surfaces together. Although waterproof and fairly durable, they can break down when exposed to frequent washing in hot water. Being reversible, they are good for repairing many collectors' display items.

The best-known brands are UHU All Purpose clear adhesive, Bostik All Purpose clear adhesive and Gloy Household Adhesive; they are all widely available.

Animal glue (also known as pearl, carpenter's or Scotch glue)
Until the arrival of plastics, all glues were made from natural materials such as animal bones and skins, starch, fish offal and the sap of trees. These traditional materials were used in the construction of all furniture, at least until the First World War. Animal glue should still be used for most kinds of woodwork and particularly for furniture repairs. It can be dissolved with warm water.

The glue has to be prepared in a water-jacketed gluepot,

and it must not be allowed to boil or it will turn dark and stain the wood. The glue is obtained in pearl or jelly form; the pearls must be soaked in cold water overnight to swell and soften them. Ensure that there is water in the outer container before placing the glue in the inner pot and heating it. The heated glue should be thin enough to run off the brush, the last drop returning to the brush. It should be applied to warmed wood in a pleasantly warm workshop. Allow up to twenty-four hours for drying.

Animal glue (and gluepots) can be found in good hardware and DIY shops, or from the specialist suppliers to the woodwork trade.

Cellulose nitrate adhesive
HMG is a multi-purpose adhesive, reversible with acetone, that can be used for wood, metal, ivory, glass, pottery and other porous substances (but not rubber).

It can be obtained from Conservation Resources*.

Cyanoacrylate adhesives (superglues)
These are the fastest setting and least reversible of glues, and should only be used on serviceable rather than precious items. Great care must be taken to avoid skin contact as they can weld fingers together as well as metals and ceramics. However, they make virtually invisible repairs to clean breaks in glass, ceramics and other hard materials. Some use the ultra-violet element in daylight to harden them, and will set more quickly in bright sunlight than on a dull day; they will not dry at all in artificial light containing no ultra-violet rays.

Before gluing, make sure the surfaces are clean, dry and close-fitting; if in doubt, swab them with methylated spirit or acetone. First, shield the pieces from the light before applying the adhesive very sparingly to only one of the surfaces to be joined. Bring the two surfaces together, accurately positioned, and then expose the mend to strong light. Excess glue can be wiped away with tissue moistened with methylated spirit or acetone; once dry, it can be pared away with a sharp blade.

Superglues like Loctite are widely available from stationers and DIY shops; a thin version, marketed as Zap, can be found in modelmakers' suppliers.

Epoxy resins

These glues are supplied in twin tubes, one of adhesive and the other of hardener; they have to be mixed thoroughly before application. Two sorts are available: those taking about six to twelve hours to set and the quick-drying varieties which will harden in about five minutes. They are especially useful for restoring ceramics as they can be turned into a filling putty by adding kaolin or titanium oxide, and they can be tinted with powder colours. Small parts can be modelled from epoxy resin putty or from epoxy resin adhesives mixed with other substances (see **Fillers**). They can be used to mend stonework, but always test porous materials first, to make sure the glue will not cause discoloration. Epoxy resins will even stick metals provided that they are thoroughly degreased and the surfaces roughened to give a key.

Before setting they can be removed with acetone: once set, try a dichloromethane-based paint remover such as Nitromors.

Among the best-known brands are Araldite and Bison Combi Standard (slow-setting); Araldite Rapid, Bison Combi Rapid and Gloy Fast Set Epoxy (fast-setting). All these are available from DIY shops, ironmongers and stationers.

Pastes

These are usually based on starch, cellulose or PVA and are water-soluble. Most commercial wallpaper pastes and some bookbinders' pastes contain a fungicide. They are suitable for repairs to paper and books.

Wallpaper pastes are widely available from DIY shops and ironmongers; pastes such as Gloy and Clam are sold by stationers, while other starch and PVA pastes are available from Conservation Resources*, good artists' suppliers like Green & Stone*, and bookbinders' suppliers such as Shepherds*.

PVA (poly vinyl acetate) emulsions

These behave in much the same way as animal glues, and are not waterproof, which means they can be dissolved with warm water. They are suitable for woodwork such as picture frames and repairs to certain materials where an easily reversible adhesive is indicated. They are applied straight from the container to both surfaces to be joined: the thinner the layer of glue, the more effective it will be. Drying takes about four hours in normal room temperatures, but joins should be held together for at least a day for maximum adhesion.

The best-known brands are Evostik Resin W, Bison Wood Glue and Unibond; Bison Extra Wood Glue is a quick-setting variety.

They are available from DIY shops, ironmongers and timber merchants.

Urea formaldehyde adhesives

Contact adhesives such as Cascamite are irreversible without damage to the object and should not be used for repairing antiques.

Adhesive tapes

Brown paper gummed tape (from stationers and artists' suppliers) should be used in preference to sticky cellulose tapes for sealing the backs of picture frames.

Masking tape is useful for temporary purposes such as masking out patterns while you are painting; drafting tape is the kind that is least likely to leave sticky marks. Another type, *Scotch Magic Tape*, is removable from paper. These should be regarded as aids to processes rather than actual repairing materials. They are available from good stationers and artists' suppliers.

Passe-partout is a strong self-adhesive binding used earlier this century as an inexpensive form of picture and photograph framing. It seems to be unavailable today and when it is indicated, for example for replacing damaged binding on lantern slides, brown paper gummed tape should be substituted.

Bleaching agents
Natural bleaching occurs from exposure to ultra-violet light, but where specific bleaching is required chemicals have to be used. Most bleaches are based on one of two principles: the decolouring and oxidizing properties of chlorine (used in most household bleaches), or oxygenated water (as in hydrogen peroxide). The strength varies, and if you need to use a bleach at all, you should start with the mildest and work towards stronger solutions only after careful testing.

Acetic acid, or white vinegar in its best-known form, is a relatively mild bleaching agent which can be used on furniture and metalwork.

Ammonia is a gas, highly soluble in water and normally sold as a solution. Household ammonia is a ten per cent solution, and the strongest solution commercially available is known as eight-eighty ammonia as it has 880 volume of the gas dissolved in one volume of water. Until recently it was used as a chemical colorant of wood, particularly mahogany, but today it is most commonly used to remove grease and dirt from glass and china, and to remove milk and casein paints from old furniture as these are impervious to most paint strippers. It may be useful for cleaning ormolu (see **Metal cleaners**). Ammonia gives off highly irritating fumes and should be used in a well-ventilated place, with protection for the skin, nose and eyes. It is available from chemists and ironmongers.

Chloramine T is a whitish powder used for bleaching paper, generally in a dilution of half an ounce to a pint of distilled water, made up just before use. It is available from Bell & Croyden* and from Conservation Resources*.

Household bleaches such as Brobat or Milton have a negligible use in restoring antiques and can do much harm.

Oxalic acid, sold in the form of white crystals and available from wood-finishing specialists, is a strong and effective (but poisonous) remover of stains like ink from wood, and can be used as a decolorant for timber, for example for matching in a repair. For stain removal dissolve one heaped tablespoon in a quart of hot water and pour some of the solution on to the stain. Before it has a chance to run over the edge, scrub it into the surface with a pad of wire wool, working in the direction of the grain. In order to avoid having a lighter area where the stain once was, an application of oxalic acid may have to be made over the complete surface, but obviously most of the rubbing will be concentrated in areas of staining. Once you have reduced the stain sufficiently (you may not be able to eradicate it completely), stop rubbing and allow the surface to remain wet for a few minutes. Before it dries out wash it over well with plenty of clean water and allow it to dry. This will take at least twenty-four hours even though it may look dry in a much shorter time. The surface will then be ready for the application of new stain and/or polish.

Hydrogen peroxide is the most commonly used bleaching agent of the oxygenating variety. It is sold in different strengths, the most common being 10 volume (this refers to the quantity of free oxygen it produces); stronger solutions are available from trade suppliers like Walsh*. However, the higher volume strengths only accelerate oxidization, and lesser strengths are safer to use.

Steradent, the denture cleaner (from chemists), has a mildly bleaching action on stained teapots and decanters.

Casting and modelling materials

The technique of casting is useful for replacing broken decoration on such items as picture frames, as long as a sufficient area of the original remains from which to make the mould. This can be done with plasticine or dental alginate. To make a plasticine mould, first warm the plasticine in a cool oven for a few minutes (to about 50°C) to soften it, and then apply it firmly to the decoration; allow it to cool and harden slightly before removing it. Finer detail and undercut patterns can be cast more successfully with dental alginate (available from the Dental Directory*). Mix it according to the instructions supplied and apply it to the pattern; it goes off quickly but remains floppy unless supported with a stiff base of plaster of Paris bandage (applied to the back of the alginate while in place on the pattern). Once the plaster of Paris backing is firm, remove the whole mould.

Plaster casts can be taken from moulds made of plasticine or dental alginate. Pour plaster of Paris or the finer dental plaster into the mould, taking care that no air bubbles are trapped in it. Once dry, remove the cast from the mould and flatten the back to a suitable depth by a combination of cutting and sandpapering. Details of undercutting or poorly moulded areas can also be carved in the hardened plaster. Once it is thoroughly dry, glue the new section of decoration on with PVA or HMG.

Silicone rubbers can also be used for casting and moulding, but they are expensive: Tiranti* will advise on their use.

Useful modelling materials include Das clay (from artists' suppliers) mixed with PVA (see FRAMES), and the epoxy putties Milliput and Sylmasta which can be filed, carved and sanded when dry. You can make your own epoxy resin putty with an epoxy resin adhesive mixed with a powder such as kaolin, fuller's earth, french chalk or titanium white; the putty can be coloured with pigment (see also **Fillers**).

Chain burnishers

These are squares of chain-mail the size of the palm of the hand, attached to a leather backing. They can be useful for burnishing iron and steel implements, and for producing a 'distressed' effect on oak and other furniture.

Colouring agents

Acrylic paints are plastic based, water soluble and therefore reversible, and are useful for many tinting and touching-up jobs.

Enamel paints are refined oil paints with a matt or gloss finish used for touching up metals and sometimes other materials. They are available in small quantities from model shops as well as art suppliers (Humbrol, Compucolor or Precision).

Gold leaf is real gold in very fine sheets; *Schlag* (Dutch metal) is a less expensive alternative. Both are available from good artists' suppliers or from Ploton* and Stuart Stevenson*.

Oil colours, or ordinary artist's oil paints, are slow-drying. Mixed with linseed oil they give a shinier finish; with turpentine a duller one.

Pigment colours are pure ground colours used for mixing into artist's colours.

Poster or powder colours are mixed with water and can also be used for tinting and touching up.

Tempera, made from ground pigments mixed with egg yolk and water, was one of the earliest painting media.

Watercolours are made from pigments mixed with gum and water. They are the most fragile of all paints.

Black lead (Zebrite) is used for blackening and polishing iron, and is available from hardware shops and ironmongers.

See also **Wood stains**.

Dry cleaners

Fuller's earth is a type of powdered clay which absorbs oils and greasy substances. It is used commercially for cleaning fabrics and furs where washing or wetting is inadvisable, and it can be effective for cleaning carpets (see CARPETS AND RUGS). *Kaolin* (china clay) has similar characteristics and can be used in the same ways. Both fuller's earth and kaolin can be used as thickeners in epoxy resin fillers (see **Fillers**).

Magnesium carbonate is a white grime-absorbing powder, useful for cleaning jewellery where wetting processes are inappropriate, and for hair on dolls.

Sodium bicarbonate (baking powder) is an alkaline powder which can be used for cleaning textiles and other materials like canework.

Bran can be heated and used for cleaning hair on dolls or taxidermy specimens.

All these substances are available from chemists.

Fillers

Fillers and stoppers are used to fill cracks and smooth out irregularities in all kinds of surfaces.

Brummer stopper is a compound formulated in various colours especially for use in cabinet making. It is smooth, can be thinned with water, and does not shrink on drying. Available from DIY shops and ironmongers, it is useful for filling cracks and small holes in furniture and papier mâché.

Chemical Metal and *Kneadable Steel* (Bison) are useful fillers for metalwork, stone and ceramics. They do not dry too hard and can be rubbed down for painting and varnishing. They are reversible with acetone or Nitromors (green tin).

Metalux wood filler can be used in the repair of ceramic dolls.

Dental plaster is a superior version of plaster of Paris, and is sometimes used for repairing ceramics. Its main use is for mending gesso-based frames, as it is an ideal material for casting replacement pieces of carving and patterned borders. It is destroyed by water. It is available from the Dental Directory* (or ask your dentist).

Epoxy resin putty (Milliput and Sylmasta) can be used for the repair of ceramics, and for modelling missing parts or for filling cracks and holes in stone and marble. The putty is white, but it can be tinted with acrylic colour before use, or painted when dry. You can also make your own putty with epoxy resin adhesive (see **Adhesives**) mixed with french chalk, kaolin, fuller's earth or, if the body of the object you are repairing is brilliant white, with titanium oxide (from art shops). Small chips and holes are easy to fill and model but larger areas of repair will need support while the putty is drying. All these are available from good art and craft suppliers such as Alec Tiranti*, Green & Stone*, Stewart Stevenson* or Hobby Aids*, who are also helpful with advice on using them.

Gesso is sometimes used as a filler as well as a base coat for surfaces to be gilded or painted (see GESSO). A thick gesso mixture can be used in successive coats to build up broken or missing areas of decoration. Repaired areas should be slightly proud of the rest of the detail to allow for rubbing down when thoroughly dry. Where original gesso has become detached or loose, new gesso can be worked underneath with a palette knife and cracks can be similarly filled. The repair will dry marble-hard and can be sand-papered or carved down to shape. Ready-prepared gesso is available in art shops.

Grain fillers can be bought in both paste and liquid forms from DIY and hardware shops and are used for making coarse-grained wood smooth before staining and finishing.

Hard wax fillers are useful for filling minor cracks caused by shrinkage in old furniture as they can be used without disturbance to the surface patination. Hard waxes in sticks of various colours, similar to sealing wax, are made by Liberon*. To use them, heat the tang of a file or other pointed tool and melt the wax by holding it on the hot metal and allowing it to run down and off the point into the crack. After hardening off, but before the wax is completely cold, trim it off with a chisel.

Paste fillers can be used for a variety of purposes, but those with plastics added tend to set rock hard and are almost irreversible. The original interior variety of Polyfilla (from DIY shops) is the best one to use, and it can be stained or painted to match its surroundings.

Plaster of Paris was used as a wood filler during the last century, but is now more often used, like dental plaster, for repairing carved details (see **Casting and modelling materials**).

Sawdust and carpenter's glue, mixed to a mastic consistency, can be used to fill quite large holes in damaged woodwork. Use sawdust of the same variety of wood as the rest of the work to make the repair less visible. Plastic Wood is a commercially available version (from DIY shops).

French polish
There are dozens of grades and qualities of french polish on the market. Many are available from DIY shops, while others are available from specialist suppliers to the furniture trade like Fiddes*, Mylands*, Bolloms* or Wastnage*. See FURNITURE *Polishing*.

Fungicides
Fungus attack is almost always associated with damp conditions and can occur in a wide variety of hosts from paper to stonework. Elimination involves removing the cause of the moisture as well as exterminating the spores. Selecting a suitable fungicide depends on the fragility of the object under attack; killing the fungus does not automatically cure the stains it has caused.

Dichlorophen, marketed as Panacide, can be used on

stone, plaster and similar materials as a fungicide for fungi, lichen and algae. It is available from hardware and DIY shops.

Mystox LPL, a concentrated oil soluble in white spirit, is a fungicide, bactericide and insecticide in one product that is not toxic to humans or pets. Its effects last for several years and it is suitable for textiles, leather, natural fibres and wood; available only from Picreator Enterprises*.

Chloramine T can be used on paper (see PAPER) and is available from Bell & Croyden* and Conservation Resources*.

Furniture cleaners

The simplest polish reviver is paraffin, wiped on with a soft rag. This will clean off some of the accumulated dirt and old wax and leave no oily solids behind. An alternative for smeary surfaces is vinegar and warm water, followed by a burnishing with a chamois leather.

Furniture polishes

Solid polishes containing beeswax are recommended for antique furniture in preference to those containing emulsifiers or silicones. Goddard's Antiquax, Johnson Wax, Liberon Waxes and Ronuk Wax Polish are all available from hardware shops; Wastnage*, Fiddes* and Mylands* are among the specialist firms that produce their own. Alternatively you can make up a traditional wax polish. Shred about a pound of beeswax and pack lightly into a double boiler. Add sufficient real turpentine to just cover the lightly packed flakes of wax and a salt-spoonful of carbon or ivory black for each pint or pound of mixture. Heat slowly, stirring occasionally and, when the mixture becomes liquid, pour it into a container to cool and harden. It should be soft enough for you to indent the finished polish with your finger.

Microcrystalline wax polish (Renaissance wax) is the

choice of professional restorers and conservators. It gives furniture a lustrous durable finish which leaves no sticky residue, does not show fingermarks and can be used on all kinds of surfaces besides wood. It is made and marketed by Picreator Enterprises*.

Humidification

Most antiques will live happily in an atmosphere of between fifty and sixty per cent relative humidity. Mould growth and corrosion of metals are likely above seventy per cent, while many materials will shrink and become brittle in levels below forty per cent.

Humidifiers have a place in the general protection of furniture and objects in dry climates or centrally heated rooms. At one end of the scale, containers of water hung on radiators, houseplants and vases of flowers may have a mildly beneficial effect, while at the other there is a range of electrical humidifying equipment. Advice on the correct appliances for particular situations is offered by the Air Improvement Centre* and Preservation Equipment*.

Insecticides

Infestations of insects can usually be controlled with the sorts of insecticides that are on sale in chemists and hard-ware shops; some of them have long-lasting effects but most are in some degree toxic to humans. *Mystox* (see **Fungicides**) is a non-toxic and highly effective fungicide, bactericide and insecticide, and is to be preferred. Another safe and effective means of pest eradication for wood, leather and some other materials is *Thermo Lignum** warm air treatment. For other types of fumigation consult your local authority pest control officer or the Conservation Unit of the Museums and Galleries Commission*. Insecticides for home use come in various forms, and their toxicity varies: they should be used with care and in accordance with the manufacturer's directions.

Dusting powders can be effective for spreading underneath carpets and rugs. They contain small percentages of active ingredient mixed with inert powder.

Mothballs and crystals, based on paradichlorobenzene, are useful for protecting clothes and fabrics in drawers and cupboards, and for scattering along the backs of bookshelves, but they should not come into direct contact with precious objects.

Dichlorvos strips (Vapona or Boots' own brand) can be hung in cupboards and other storage areas as a repellent and insecticide, but their vapour is toxic so they should not be used in the living areas of houses.

Low Odour Cuprinol or *Rentokil*, available from chemists and hardware shops, are effective insecticides for woodworm, which attacks woods such as walnut, beech and pine but not mahogany, teak and oak heartwood. Little piles of sawdust in the springtime are a sign of infestation by the larva of the furniture beetle. The adult insect lays its eggs on suitable end-grain or other wood where they hatch into minute caterpillars which bore their way into the timber, forming tube-like galleries. Eventually they pupate just below the surface, waiting for spring when they hatch into adult beetles which bite their way out, leaving neat round exit holes. The adult insect lives for only a few days, so permanent protection is easy with a long-lasting insecticide which is both poisonous to the feeding grub and repellent to the adult female (who will not lay eggs on treated wood).

The best time for treatment is early spring, before the beetles emerge, but any time will do. The chemical comes in a solution which will not harm furniture. Apply by brush or spray, taking care to treat all surfaces, both interior and exterior. There will probably be an emergence of beetles the following spring, because the insecticide will not penetrate all the galleries, but this does not mean that the treatment has not been effective.

Leather treatments

Pliantine (British Museum Leather Dressing) is a good general dressing for leathers, while *Vulpex* spirit soap is a useful cleaner. *Pliantex* may be used to consolidate roughened leather surfaces. All three are available from Conservation Resources*; Vulpex is also supplied by Picreator Enterprises* who produce their own dressing, *Renaissance Leather Reviver*. *Connolly's Hide Food* (from saddlers) can be used on robust leathers. For a protective surface coating use *SC6000* (from the Leather Conservation Centre*) or Renaissance microcrystalline wax polish. *Saddle soap*, used with small quantities of water, has a cleansing as well as a polishing action but should only be used on such items as military accoutrements, luggage and, of course, saddles (see LEATHER).

Light protection

Damage to objects by light is mainly due to ultra-violet rays, and various filters and barriers can be used on window panes, fluorescent tubes and lamps. Infra-red rays are also damaging, and cool-beam spotlights, which reflect the infra-red beams backwards, can help to reduce the risk to specific objects. Fibre-optic lighting, which produces minimal heat, is to be preferred to incandescent lights. As a general precaution against light damage, curtains should be drawn in sunny rooms when they are not in use, and vulnerable objects should be displayed (if at all) in well-shaded areas or on dark walls.

Protective equipment is available from Conservation Resources* and Preservation Equipment*.

Metal cleaners and polishes

It is important to remember that all metal-cleaning processes, by the action of rubbing, remove fractional amounts of the metallic surface: the more abrasive the process, the more the metal will be diminished, so the best policy is to clean rarely and with the least abrasive method that will succeed. The use of Renaissance microcrystalline wax polish to protect metal surfaces from tarnishing and damaging pollutants, and thus reduce the need for frequent cleaning, is recommended.

Having said that, *Brasso*, *Duraglit* and *Silver Dip* are all useful and widely available cleaners (see the entries for specific metals for their appropriate uses); use separate waddings, solutions, brushes and cloths for different metals.

Paraffin oil, on fine wire wool, can be used for cleaning iron and steel, while corroded pewter can be soaked in it. Do not allow paraffin or paraffin oil to come into contact with plastic or rubber (see IRON AND STEEL, PEWTER and **Rust removers**).

Prelim is a specially formulated paste for cleaning metals of all kinds without scratching them; it is said to be suitable even for gilded surfaces, and is widely used by conservators. It is available from Picreator Enterprises* and Conservation Resources*.

Polishing with long-term products such as Goddard's *Long Term Silver Polish*, *Long Term Silver Foam* or *Long Term Copper and Brass Cleaner* helps to reduce the frequency of cleaning as they contain chemical tarnish barriers.

Iron and steel can be polished with jeweller's emery paper, rouge powder and other compounds available from specialists like H. S. Walsh*, but the mildly abrasive Prelim and the chrome cleaner, *Solvol Autosol* (see **Abrasives**), are particularly useful as they can be used for many other materials too.

Corrosion on iron, copper and bronze can be removed with *Biox* conservation liquid (from Conservation Resources*) or *Renaissance Metal De-corroder* (from Picreator Enterprises*). The latter can also be used on brass, steel, zinc and galvanized materials. Use *jeweller's rouge and salad oil*, or *Goddard's Glow* for pewter, and *Silver Dip* for Britannia metal.

Ormolu can be cleaned with *Vulpex* liquid soap with warm or cold water (in a five per cent solution). Ammonia treatment for ormolu should be avoided if possible and only undertaken with extreme care. Always remove the ormolu mounts from their base first. The following recipe is suitable for ormolu and other metals and it also removes old lacquer. Half fill a one-gallon ice-cream tub with hot water and whisk in soft soap until well mixed. Fill it up with cold water to within half a pint of the top and, when the water is cool, add half a pint of ammonia, keeping well clear of the fumes. Put the lid on the mixture to prevent evaporation. Soak the pieces in the solution until the dirt begins to come off: this may take as little as five minutes or as much as forty-five (lacquered pieces take longer). Brush the mounts gently to remove all traces of dirt and then remove them from the pickle and wash thoroughly under very hot water to remove all traces of the ammonia mixture; if necessary use a soft toothbrush in the crevices. Dry carefully with a clean tea towel or in box dust (available from jewellery equipment suppliers).

See also separate headings on metals for specific advice on cleaning them.

Microcrystalline wax polish
This hard, semi-synthetic wax, marketed as Renaissance Wax, polishes to a glass-clear, smooth, non-sticky finish and is an invaluable protection against damp, dirt and pollution for all kinds of materials. For best results apply sparingly to small sections at a time and polish immediately. Renaissance Wax Polish is manufactured and supplied by Picreator Enterprises*; it is also available from Conservation Resources* and some retail shops.

Non-ionic detergent
The recommended *Synperonic N* (available from Conservation Resources*) is a soapy cleaning substance that contains

no chemicals, unlike household detergents. Although its action is relatively weak, it is very concentrated and a few drops in lukewarm water are enough for most jobs. Fairy Liquid is the household washing-up liquid containing the fewest chemicals, so it could be used as an alternative in some cases. Mild washing substances such as Stergene, Woolite and Dreft are safer for textiles than others.

Oils and lubricants

Linseed oil is one of the traditional materials for dressing and polishing wood. Throughout the eighteenth century the standard practice was to impregnate wood with a mixture of linseed oil and turpentine and burnish the surface with fine brick dust on a cork rubber. Mixed with shellac it was the basis of 'coach varnish'. It is used these days as a reviver and ring remover on antique furniture, and as a dressing for garden furniture made from raw unpainted timber. The practice of using a drop or two when applying the finishing coat of french polish is to be discouraged as it reduces the hardness of the surface. It is available from ironmongers and artists' suppliers.

Molybdenum disulphide (Dri-Slide) is a non-oily lubricant, good for protecting steel and other metal moving parts where an excess of oil is undesirable. It is used mostly for sporting guns but is useful for the general protection of armour and weapons. It is available from gunsmiths. The non-oily, non-greasy Renaissance microcrystalline wax polish is also an excellent protection for metalwork.

Penetrating oils have two main uses: loosening hard-to-shift nuts, bolts and screws, and lifting rust and corrosion. The simplest all-round kind is *paraffin oil*, but after its use for removing rust, the object must be oiled to prevent more rust forming. More sophisticated penetrating oils, such as *Plus Gas* and *WD40*, available from hardware and motor accessory shops, are invaluable in a restorer's workshop.

Rifle oil or *Rangoon oil* is the traditional oil used on

firearms to keep them rust free and in good working order. Others, such as *3-0-3*, *3-in-1*, *sewing machine oil* and *silicone gun oil 35* are good alternatives. Do not use motor or heavy lubricating oils on fine machinery as they are liable to gum parts up.

Most of these oils are available from gunsmiths or hardware shops; sewing machine oil from haberdashers and fabric shops.

Turpentine is the natural oily sap of certain types of pine tree. Although no longer used for mixing commercial paints, it is still used for thinning and mixing artist's oil colours, and in wax furniture polishes.

Paint strippers

Nitromors is the most effective and widely available stripper on the market. Two varieties are on sale: that in the green tin will remove plastic paints and hard enamels, and will dissolve many adhesives, while the type in the yellow tin is suitable for the removal of varnish and french polish. Nitromors (like some other paint strippers) is based on dichloromethane (methylene chloride) which is highly toxic and should be used in a well-ventilated place (outside if possible) well away from fires or smokers. Wear rubber gloves and goggles.

The effectiveness of strippers is greatly enhanced by using the correct technique. Those unfamiliar with stripping paintwork from wood commonly make the mistake of applying the stripper as if it were paint, brushing it out to produce a smooth surface. This reduces the efficiency of the stripper and results in a need for more coats. Apply as much of the stripper to the surface as will stick, and leave it until the varnish, polish or paint has started to swell and cockle.

Remove the first layer or so with a metal scraper, taking care not to damage the surface of the wood. Several applications of stripper will be needed to remove every vestige of the finish, and it is important that the object is absolutely clear if you are going to repolish it. In the final stages of stripping, the scraper should be replaced with a ball of coarse wire wool, used in the direction of the grain. Carving and awkward corners are best cleaned with a combination of wire wool and pointed pieces of scrap wood that will reach into the crevices. After stripping is finished, neutralize the residue of the chemical by wiping the surface with white spirit.

Modern paint strippers will remove nearly every kind of finish with the exception of milk paint (see FURNITURE *Painted furniture*) which is impervious to most paint strippers and in any case should probably be left alone. It is likely to respond only to strong ammonia. This has to be scrubbed in with wire wool and left to soak. The resulting treacly mass can be washed and scraped off, again using wire wool to remove the last vestige.

Rust removers
Paraffin oil, applied with fine wire wool, is a traditional method of cleaning rust off iron and steel, but the surfaces should be re-oiled afterwards to prevent more rust forming. Commercial products such as *Jenolite* (from car spares shops and ironmongers) and *Modalene* (from Catomance*), based on phosphoric acid, destroy and remove rust, leaving behind a coating of inert iron phosphate which is a positive corrosion inhibitor, but they can be harsh in their action. They are available in both liquid and jelly form for either brush or spot application. *Renaissance Metal Decorroder* (from Picreator Enterprises*) and *Biox Conservation Liquid* (from Conservation Resources*) are specially formulated for the conservation of antique metals (see **Metal cleaners and polishes**).

Silicone paper and waxed paper
These are non-stick papers of particular usefulness in gluing tasks. They are available from artists' suppliers. Waxed paper has lower heat resistance.

Solvents

Generally speaking, solvents are liquids that can be used to loosen or wash off all kinds of dirt and grease. They include water as well as many of the substances we have discussed under separate headings, but here we include other volatile liquids that have specific uses. They should all be available from chemists.

Acetone is a rapid solvent of varnishes, cellulose paints, plastics and some glues (see **Adhesives**) and is useful as a general cleaning fluid. It is highly flammable and should be used in well-ventilated conditions as the vapour is dangerous to inhale.

Alcohol in the form of *methylated spirit* (alcohol debased with dye and other noxious substances to make it undrinkable), colourless *surgical spirit* or *isopropyl alcohol* is used for removing grease, oil and grime, or for general cleaning when water would be damaging. It can be mixed with water for accelerated drying and the removal of moisture, and is the basic solvent in french polish. It will dissolve french-polished and some varnished surfaces. To avoid staining, use uncoloured surgical spirit.

Carbon tetrachloride is a solvent mainly used in commercial dry cleaning. Although non-flammable, it produces poisonous fumes near naked flames or cigarettes and should only be used in well-ventilated conditions. It is rarely of use in cleaning antique objects or materials.

White spirit, also known as *turps substitute* or *odourless kerosene*, is widely used as a dry-cleaning substance, mixed with more volatile solvents; it will not mix with water. White spirit is safer to use than most other solvents, but it can burn. It will not damage french polish or varnish, but will dissolve waxes, so can be useful as a furniture cleaner in certain circumstances. A mixture of equal quantities of white spirit and paraffin is a highly effective and safe degreasant, used with care.

Varnishes and lacquers

Many surfaces benefit from a coating of varnish or lacquer, giving protection against damp, dirt and pollution as well as wear and tear. For painted wood surfaces such as penwork, early forms of Tunbridge ware or painted furniture, and for papier mâché and oil paintings, use a light retouching varnish, available from artists' suppliers. Easy to use, it is thin and quick-drying, and can be removed with white spirit.

Polished metalwork can be protected with *Frigilene*, a cellulose nitrate lacquer for silver and plated wares, or *Ercalene*, a clear lacquer containing a corrosion inhibitor for copper, brass and bronze. They are available from H. S. Walsh* and Conservation Resources*. Alternatively, use *Joy Transparent Paint*, suitable for all non-ferrous metals and available from hardware shops and ironmongers. It should be thinned with a cellulose thinner and applied on a well-charged brush; work in a warm room.

Lacquer on metals may eventually turn dark or begin to peel off. In this case it needs to be removed and replaced. Always detach fittings such as brass handles from furniture before cleaning off the lacquer. Many lacquers can be removed with acetone or Nitromors (wash the object well in running water afterwards), or use the recipe for cleaning ormolu (see **Metal cleaners**).

Wood stains

Most *traditional water-based wood stains* had a chemical as well as a colouring action. Water stains have the disadvantage of being slow to dry and of raising the grain of the wood; they require experience to manage successfully. Their advantage is that they are fast, non-fading colours.

Ammonia imparts a rich red colour to mahogany and some other woods; these days it is applied in liquid form rather than the traditional fuming. *Brunswick* produces a variety of pinks and scarlets, depending on the strength of the solution. *Caustic soda* turns pine and some other light woods greyish and produces a mid-brown in elm and oak. *Potassium bichromate*, though naturally orange, has a chemical action which, on most furniture woods, develops to a honey-brown after an hour or so. *Turmeric* is a yellow stain. *Vandyke crystals* produce a cold dark brown. There are many others; varying tones can be shaded in with pigments such as lamp black and red lead.

Aniline dyes, used in naphtha or methylated spirit, are ready-mixed stains that are quick and easy for the amateur to use, but are more likely to fade and alter in colour than the water-based stains; they can cause particular problems with walnut and satinwood. Colours range from golden oak to brown walnut and dark oak. Do not be misled by these wood names: they are merely descriptive labels for identifying colours and the dyes can be used on all kinds of woods. Start with a light shade and work the wood up to the colour you want by multiple applications of various shades of stain.

Pigments and powder colours are useful for making up more concentrated solutions for painting in grain configurations, dark patches or shading where the ready-made stains do not give the desired effect.

Wood stains are available in many DIY and ironmongers' shops, at timber merchants, or from specialist suppliers like Liberon*, Myland*, Bollom*, Wastnage* and Fiddes*.

Section Three
Directory of Suppliers and Organizations

SUPPLIERS
Air Improvement Centre
23 Denbigh Street
London SW1V 2HF
0171 834 2834   Humidifiers

Aldrich Chemicals
The Old Brickyard
New Road
Gillingham
Dorset SP8 4JL
01747 822211   Conservation chemicals

Alma
Unit D
12–14 Greatorex Street
London E1 5NF
0171 375 0343   Leathers

Antique Leathers Ltd
4 Park End
South Hill Park
London NW3 2SE
0171 435 8582   Table leathers

Ashley Iles (Edge Tools) Ltd
East Kirkby
Spilsby
Lincolnshire PE23 4DD
01790 763372   Carving tools and chisels

Atlantis European Ltd
146 Brick Lane
London E1 6RU
0171 377 8855   Art materials and papers

Battle Hayward & Bower Ltd
Crofton Drive
Allenby Road Industrial Estate
Lincoln LN3 4NP
01522 529206   Soft soap

W. Beal & Partners
Unit 44 Pembroke Centre
Cheney Manor
Swindon
Wiltshire SN2 2PQ
01793 511920   Table leathers

J. D. Beardmore
3–4 Percy Street
London W1P 0EJ
0171 637 7041   Brass handles and fittings

A. Bell & Co. Ltd
Kingsthorpe Road
Northampton NN2 6LT
01604 712505   Stone-cleaning materials

John Bell & Croyden Ltd
50–54 Wigmore Street
London W1H 0AU
0171 935 5555   Chloramine T and other chemicals

Bolloms (incorporating Henry Flack)
PO Box 78
Croydon Road
Beckenham
Kent BR3 4BL
0181 658 2299   Wood-finishing materials

Catomance plc (incorporating Modastic Ltd)
96 Bridge Road East
Welwyn Garden City
Hertfordshire AL7 1JW
0170 7324373   Modalene

Classic Collection
2 Pied Bull Yard
Bury Place
London WC1A 2JR
0171 831 6000   Repairs to vintage cameras

Conservation Resources
Unit 1
Pony Road
Horspath Industrial Estate
Cowley
Oxford OX4 2RD
01865 747755   Conservation supplies

Crispin & Son Ltd
92 Curtain Road
London EC2A 3AA
0171 739 4857   Stringing wood, veneers and inlays

The Dental Directory
6 Perry Way
Witham
Essex CM8 3SX
01376 500222   Dental alginate and dental plaster

The Dolls' House
Market Place
Northleach
Gloucestershire GL54 3EJ
01451 860431   Dolls' house supplies

Ellis & Farrier Ltd
20 Beak Street
London W1R 3HA   Beads, sequins, braids,
0171 629 9964   feathers, jewellery findings

Falkiner Fine Papers
76 Southampton Row
London WC1N 3XX   Papers for art and
0171 831 1151   conservation

The Fan Museum
12 Crooms Hill
Greenwich SE10 8QN
0181 305 1441   Fan-repairing supplies

Fiddes & Son
Florence Works
Brindley Road
Cardiff CF1 7TX
01222 340323   Wood-finishing materials

The Glass Dome Company
62 Priory Road
Tonbridge
Kent TN9 2BL
01732 360830   Glass domes, bases and display cases

Green & Stone
259 King's Road
London SW3 5EL   Art, craft, restoration and
0171 352 6521   gilding supplies and materials

Keith Harding's World of Mechanical Music
The Oak House
High Street
Northleach   Supplies and services for
Gloucestershire GL54 3ET   clock, musical box and
01451 860181   automata repairs

Hobby Aids
PO Box 262
Haywards Heath
West Sussex RH16 3FR
01444 415027   China repair supplies

Hobby Horse
15–17 Langton Street
London SW10 0JL
0171 351 1913   Beads, sequins and jewellery findings

W. S. Jenkins Ltd
Tariff Road
London N17 0EN
0181 808 2336   Wood-finishing materials

John Lawrence & Co. Ltd
Granville Street
Dover
Kent CT16 2LF
01304 201425   Brass handles and fittings

The Leather Conservation Centre
34 Guildhall Road
Northampton NN1 1EW   Leather conservation
01604 23272   supplies; SC6000

Le Ronka
84 Vyse Street
Hockley
Birmingham B18 6HA
0121 551 3785   Jewellery repair supplies

Liberon Waxes Ltd
Mountfield Industrial Estate
Learoyd Road
New Romney
Kent TN28 8XU
01797 367555   Furniture repair materials

The London Dolls' House Company
29 Covent Garden Market
London WC2E 8RE
0171 240 8681   Dolls' house supplies

Mace & Nairn
89 Crane Street
Salisbury
Wiltshire
SP1 2PY
01722 336903   Embroidery and lacemaking supplies

Meadows & Passmore
Farningham Road
Crowborough
East Sussex TN6 2JP
01892 662255   Parts for clocks and barometers

John Myland Ltd
80 Norwood High Street
West Norwood
London SE27 9NW
0181 670 9161   Wood-finishing materials

Parry Tyzack Ltd
329 Old Street
London EC1V 9LQ
0171 739 8301   Hand, power and machine tools

Picreator Enterprises
44 Park View Gardens
Hendon NW4 2PN
0181 202 8972   Conservation materials

E. Ploton Ltd
273 Archway Road
London N6 5AA
0181 348 2838   Gilding supplies

Pollock's Toy Museum
Scala Street
London W1P 1LU
0171 636 3452   Dolls' limbs, heads and eyes

Porter Nicholson
Portland House
Norlington Road
Leyton E10 6JX
0181 539 0271   Upholstery supplies

Preservation Equipment Ltd
Diss
Norfolk IP22 2DG
01379 651527   Conservation supplies and equipment

Recollect Studios
The Old School
London Road
Sayers Common
West Sussex BN6 9HX
01273 833314   Doll-repairing supplies and parts

Reeves
178 Kensington High Street
London W8 7NX   General crafts suppliers,
0171 937 5370   including papers, cane, etc.

H. E. Saville
9 St Martin's Place
Scarborough
North Yorkshire YO11 2QH
01723 373032   Brass handles and fittings

Shepherds
76B Rochester Row
London SW1P 1JU
0171 630 1184   Bookbinding supplies and service

The Singing Tree
69 New King's Road
London SW6 4SQ
0171 736 4527   Dolls' house supplies

J. Smith & Sons (Clerkenwell) Ltd
42–56 Tottenham Road
London N1 4BZ
0171 253 1277   Brass inlay, strip and sheet

Specialist Crafts (formerly Dryad)
PO Box 247
Leicester LE1 9QS   General craft supplies, including
0116 2510405   cane, seagrass, etc.

Specialist Supplies Ltd
The Yard
Dereham
Norfolk NR19 2BP
01362 694165   Clock and barometer parts

Stuart R. Stevenson
68 Clerkenwell Road
London EC1M 5QA   Art and craft supplies, especially
0171 253 1693   gilding and china restoration

Thermo Lignum UK Ltd
Unit 19
Grand Union Centre
West Row
Ladbroke Grove
London W10 5AS
0181 964 3964   Pest eradication

Alec Tiranti Ltd
70 High Street
Theale
Reading RG7 5AR
01734 302775
or 27 Warren Street
London W1P 5DG   Carving, moulding, casting, gilding
0171 636 8565   and general art supplies

H. S. Walsh & Sons (incorporating T. A. Hutchinson)
243 Beckenham Road
Beckenham
Kent BR3 4TS   Materials and equipment for
0181 778 7061   the metalwork trades

C. W. Wastnage Ltd
Springfield Industrial Estate
Burnham-on-Crouch
Essex
0621 785173   Wood-finishing materials

Watts & Co. Ltd
7 Tufton Street
London SW1P 3QE
0171 222 2893   Cords, braids and trimmings

Woolnough (AC) Ltd
Unit W107
Holywell Centre
Phipp Street
London EC2A 4PS
0171 739 6603   Baize and facecloth

Christopher Wray's Lighting Emporium
600 King's Road
London SW6 2DX   Lamp glasses, lighting sundries
0171 736 8434   and glass domes

ORGANIZATIONS
The Association of British Picture Restorers
Station Avenue
Kew
Surrey TW9 3QA
0181 948 5644

British Antique Dealers' Association
20 Rutland Gate
London SW7 1BD
0171 589 4128

British Antique Furniture Restorers' Association
The Old Rectory
Warmwell
Dorchester
Dorset DT2 8HQ
01305 852104

Cliveden Conservation Workshop Ltd (Stone, statuary, wall paintings, etc.)
The Tennis Courts
Cliveden Estate
Taplow
nr Maidenhead
Berkshire SL6 0JA
01628 604721

The Conservation Unit
Museums and Galleries Commission
16 Queen Anne's Gate
London SW1H 9AA
0171 233 4200

The Fan Museum
12 Crooms Hill
Greenwich SE10 8QN
0181 305 1441

The Guild of Master Craftsmen
166 High Street
Lewes
East Sussex BN7 1XU
01273 478449

The Institute of Paper Conservation
Leigh Lodge
Leigh
Worcester WR6 5LB
01886 832323

The Leather Conservation Centre
34 Guildhall Road
Northampton NN1 1EW
01604 232723

London and Provincial Antique Dealers' Association
Suite 214
535 King's Road
London SW10 0SZ
0171 823 3511

Rural Development Commission (formerly CoSIRA)
141 Castle Street
Salisbury
Wiltshire SP1 3TP
01722 336255

The Textile Conservation Centre
Apartment 22
Hampton Court Palace
East Molesey
Surrey KT8 9AU
081 977 4943

United Kingdom Institute for Conservation
6 Whitehorse Mews
Westminster Bridge Road
London SE1 7QD
0171 620 3371

West Dean College
Chichester
Sussex PO18 0QZ
01243 811301

Further reading

The Conservation Source Book (Conservation Unit, Museums and Galleries Commission, 1991)

The National Trust Manual of Housekeeping by Hermione Sandwith and Sheila Stainton (Penguin, 1984)

Looking After Antiques by Anna Plowden and Frances Halahan (Pan, 1987)

Sotheby's Caring for Antiques edited by Mette Tang Simpson and Michael Huntley (Conran Octopus, 1992)

Index

Abrasives, 16, 35, 42, 50, 138, 147–9, 165
Acetone, 37, 43, 58, 94, 151, 152, 158, 170, 171
Acrylic paint, 43, 52, 59, 97, 117, 118, 132, 139, 157, 159
Acrylic sheet, 149
Adhesive labels, removal of, 30
Adhesive pastes, 32
Adhesive tape, 32, 98, 116, 132, 137, 153, 154
Adhesives, 16, 18, 40, 41, 50, 59, 149–53, 168
Agate, 36, 86, 89
Alabaster, 15, 16, 104
Aluminium, 16
Amber, 16–18
Ambroid, 18
Ammonia, 120, 129, 154, 155, 166, 169, 171
Animal glue, 23, 33, 61, 63, 65, 69, 70, 80, 83, 140, 150, 153
Anodizing, 16
Antimony, 34
Antler, 92, 131
Araldite, 36, 43, 45, 51, 105, 145, 152
Armour, 18, 167
Art Deco, 45
Automata, 105

Babel, Peter, 116
Backus book cloth cleaner, 31
Baize, 21
Baking powder (see Sodium Bicarbonate)

Balsa wood, 52
Bamboo, 21–3
Barometers, 23–6
Basketwork, 26
Beading (furniture), 64, 66
Beads, 27, 28, 49, 95
Beadwork, 28, 29
Beeswax, 73, 100, 161
Bell's 1967 Cleaner, 15, 104, 130
Bell's marble polish, 105
Bellows, 29
Biox, 20, 165, 169
Biscuit ware (bisque), 42, 50
Bleaches, 26, 43, 77, 78, 93, 104, 114, 120, 137, 154–6
Bluejohn, 29
Bone, 26, 32, 59, 61, 69, 92–4
Bone china, 42
Books and bookbindings, 29–32, 86, 100, 118
Bostik, 16, 18, 29, 50, 59, 89, 90, 93, 94, 97, 105, 108, 113, 117, 127, 131, 150
Bottles, 87
Boulle, 32
Boulton, Matthew, 29
Bran, 56, 158
Brass, 26, 32, 33, 34, 37
Breadcrumbs, 60
Bricks, 130
Britannia metal, 34, 35, 126, 165
British Library, 32
Bronze, 35
Brummer stopper, 77, 117, 123, 141, 158
Burnishing, 76, 157

Calfskin, 59
Cameo, 36, 113
Cameras, 36, 37
Camphor crystals, 88
Canework, 37, 38, 158
Carbon tetrachloride, 49, 58, 170
Carpets, 39–41
Carving, 62, 84, 85, 94, 159
Cascamite, 153
Casting, 84, 85, 156, 157, 159
Castors, 67
Caustic soda, 71, 172
Celluloid, 50, 51, 122
Cellulose nitrate adhesive, 151
Ceramics, 36, 41–3, 158, 159
Chairs, 38
Chandeliers, 44
Chemical Metal, 43, 158
Chestnut, 13, 113
Chewing gum, 41
Chicken skin, 59
Chloramine T, 114, 115, 155, 161
Christopher Wray's Lighting
    Emporium, 44
Chromium, 44, 45, 90, 110
Clay, Henry, 116
Cleansing cream, 51
Clock cases, 15, 45
Clocks, 45–8
Cock beads, 64, 65
Coins, 4
Colouring agents, 157
Composition, 50, 51, 52, 83, 84
Connolly's Hide Food, 31, 100, 164
Copper, 33, 34, 35, 49, 129
Coral, 49, 50, 95
Corrosion, 16, 19, 20, 35, 36, 45, 47,
    98, 119, 123, 162, 165, 167
Cracks, 12, 59, 77, 84
Cramping, 65, 77
Crazing, 59
Crocus powder, 89, 119, 149
Cross-bandings, 80–2
Cuprinol, 31, 163
Cuttlefish bone, 114
Cyanoacrylate adhesives, 151

Das Clay, 84, 85, 97, 156
Deep freezing, 31, 120
Dental alginate, 84, 156
Dents, 21, 51, 67, 98, 119
Distilled water, 15, 104, 105
Dolls, 50–7, 158
Dolls' houses, 57, 58
Drawings, 114

Dubbin, 37
Dry cleaning, 56, 158

Earthenware, 42
Electro-plated wares, 34, 35, 126
Enamels, 58, 95
Enzyme gels, 72
EPNS 110
Epoxy resin adhesive, 34, 36, 43, 51,
    52, 53, 91, 94, 96, 105, 139, 152,
    156
Epoxy resin casting, 35
Epoxy resin filler, 16, 34, 43, 52, 91,
    132, 152, 158, 159
Eraser, 30, 60, 100, 114
Ercalene, 34, 171
Eros, 16
Ether, 18

Fairy Liquid, 42, 56, 167
Fan Museum, The, 61
Fans, 59
Feathers, 59, 131
Felt, 13, 51, 113, 126, 127, 135
Fillers, 57, 67, 83, 85, 132, 152,
    158–60
Foxing, 114, 115
Frames, 62, 83–5, 107, 153, 156, 158
French chalk, 18, 41, 105, 157, 159
French polish and polishing, 72–6, 97,
    160, 167, 168, 170
Fretwork, 62
Frigilene, 35, 126, 129, 171
Fuller's earth, 41, 131, 157, 158, 159
Fungicides, 31, 120, 130, 152, 160,
    161
Fur, 131
Furniture, 62–83, 161
Furniture, painted, 71, 72, 168, 169,
    171
Furniture polish, 21, 73, 161, 162

Garnet paper, 76, 83, 141, 148
Gesso, 50, 83, 84, 97, 159
Gilbert, Alfred, 16
Gilding, 42, 72, 73, 83–6, 102, 107,
    159
Glass, 18, 26, 36, 44, 58, 87–9, 106,
    107
Gloy, 150, 153
Glycerine, 33, 88
Gold, 25, 49
Gold leaf, 86, 157
Gouache, 106, 114
Guns, 18–21, 167

Gypsum, 15

Handles, 19, 34, 69, 73, 93, 94, 128, 171
Hardstones, 89
Hinges, 32, 69, 124
HMG, 16, 18, 29, 37, 50, 59, 60, 61, 84, 89, 93, 94, 97, 105, 108, 113, 117, 131, 151, 156
Hooke, Robert, 25
Holes, 40, 52, 77, 98, 105, 119
Horn, 32, 59, 89
Humidification, 63, 162
Hydrogen peroxide, 26, 43, 78, 137, 154, 155

Inks, 37, 71, 114, 141, 155
Inlays, 33, 69, 70, 78, 93, 107, 108, 121
Insecticides, 26, 111, 117, 131, 161, 162, 163
Intaglios, 36
Intarsia, 69, 70
Iron, 19, 90, 91, 98, 165
Ironing, 41
Isopropyl alcohol, 131, 170
Ivory, 26, 59, 60, 61, 69, 92–4, 95, 121

Jade, 94
Japanese tissue paper, 32, 116, 120
Japanning, 96, 117, 138
Jennens & Bettridge, 116
Jenolite, 91, 105, 138, 169
Jet, 94
Jeweller's rouge, 16, 35, 50, 89, 119, 149
Jewellery, 18, 94–6, 121, 158
Joy Transparent Paint, 34, 35, 113, 124, 171

Kaolin, 43, 105, 152, 157, 158, 159
Kilims, 39
Kneadable Steel, 34, 158
Knives, 91
Kodak Lens Cleaner, 37

Lace, 59, 60, 136, 137
Lacquer, 19, 35, 37, 59, 86, 91, 96, 113, 123, 126, 129, 171
Lantern slides, 37, 97
Lead, 34, 35, 98
Lead soldiers, 99
Leather, 19, 21, 29, 31, 37, 51, 52, 60, 86, 99–102, 124, 164

Light protection, 164
Lloyd Loom, 27
Locks, 19, 20, 102, 103
Lubrasil, 76, 148
Lubricants, 167, 168

Magic lanterns, 36, 97
Magnesium carbonate, 95, 158
Marble, 15, 104, 105, 159
Marquetry, 32, 70
Masking tape, 23, 43, 64, 124, 153
Mechanical antiques, 105
Medals, 49
Mercury, 23, 25
Metal cleaners and polishes, 33, 34, 35, 47, 49, 76, 121, 126, 128, 164, 165
Metals and metalwork, 18, 33, 44, 69, 91, 158, 171
Metalux, 52, 158
Methylated Spirit, 16, 17, 18, 21, 27, 35, 72, 88, 90, 92, 107, 127, 129, 138, 151, 152, 170, 172
Microcrystalline wax polish, 15, 16, 18, 19, 29, 33, 34, 35, 38, 50, 62, 71, 73, 86, 89, 91, 93, 94, 97, 98, 100, 105, 112, 113, 117, 119, 123, 124, 125, 138, 139, 140, 141, 145, 161, 164, 166, 167
Mildew, 31, 114
Milk paint, 71, 154, 169
Milliput, 16, 43, 52, 57, 156, 159
Miniatures, 106, 118
Mirrors, 62, 84, 106, 107
Mitring, 65
Monuments, 15
Modalene, 91, 138, 169
Modelling and moulding, 83–5, 122, 156, 157
Moth and mothproofing, 21, 31, 92, 131, 134, 163
Mother-of-pearl, 32, 59, 60, 69, 107, 121
Mystox, 31, 161, 162
Mould, 30, 31, 47, 106, 114, 120, 162
Moulding (furniture), 64, 65, 66
Musical boxes, 108–10

Necklaces, 27, 28, 95
Nickel, 110
Nickel silver, 35, 110, 126
Nitric acid, 49, 127
Nitromors, 21, 34, 43, 72, 104, 124, 140, 152, 158, 168, 171

Non-ionic detergent, 13, 26, 57, 89, 98, 104, 166, 167

Oak, 13, 98, 113, 126
Oil, linseed, 21, 76, 157, 167
Oil, lubricating, 19, 35, 37, 45, 76, 91, 93, 105, 119, 139, 165, 167
Oil paintings, 110–12, 157, 171
Oil, penetrating, 19, 20, 88, 103, 119, 124, 167
Onyx, 36, 89, 112, 113
Ormolu, 42, 73, 113, 154, 166, 171
Oxalic acid, 77, 78, 155
Oxidization, 16, 33

Paints (see Colouring agents)
Paint stripper, 21, 34, 38, 71, 72, 82, 104, 140, 168
Panacide, 160
Paper, 26, 29, 30, 59, 60, 113–16
Papier mâché, 50, 52, 61, 116, 171
Paradichlorobenzene, 31, 131, 163
Paraffin, 19, 20, 91, 103, 124, 161, 170
Parchment, 26, 59, 60, 117, 118
Parian ware, 42, 50
Parquetry, 70
Passe-partout, 97, 154
Pastes, 116, 120, 152
Patina, 35, 63, 119
Pearls, 27, 95
Penwork, 118, 171
Pewter, 34, 119, 120, 165
Photographs, 120
Pinchbeck, 121
Piqué, 59, 121
Plaster, 104, 121, 122
Plaster, dental, 158, 160
Plaster of Paris, 83, 84, 122, 156, 158, 160
Plasticine, 43, 156
Plastics, 36, 44, 50, 51, 61, 122
Plastic wood, 160
Pliantex, 99, 164
Pliantine, 31, 37, 164
Plus Gas, 20
Polish, shoe and boot, 19
Polishing and repolishing (furniture), 63
Polyfilla, 57, 97, 123, 160
Porcelain, 26, 41, 50
Portraits, 15, 36
Poster paints, 57, 85, 105, 157
Prelim, 16, 34, 35, 42, 45, 50, 90, 94, 96, 105, 139, 147, 148, 165

Prints, 114–16
Prisoner of war work, 92
Pumice powder, 33, 76, 149
PVA, 18, 23, 26, 32, 38, 51, 52, 57, 60, 61, 62, 80, 84, 90, 93, 96, 97, 100, 101, 124, 131, 140, 152, 153, 156

Rattan, 37
Recollect Studios, 50, 53
Red rot, 99
Renaissance De-corroder, 20, 37, 91, 138, 165, 169
Renaissance wax, 20, 161, 165, 166, 167
Rentokil, 31, 163
Ribbon, 60, 61
Rivets, 43, 61
Rock crystal, 36, 87
Rubber, 37, 84, 120, 126, 127, 156
Rugs, 39–41
Rural Development Commission, 27, 38
Rushwork, 122
Rust, 19, 20, 37, 44, 90, 91, 167, 169
Rustin's plastic coating, 43

Saddle soap, 99, 164
Salts, 36, 120, 127
SC 6000, 100, 164
Scagliola, 123
Schlag, 86, 157
Scientific instruments, 123, 124
Scratches, 12, 63, 88, 89, 98, 110, 119
Screens, 21, 124
Screws, 20, 63, 103, 124, 125, 167
Sculptures, 15, 16, 104
Shagreen, 125
Sheffield plate 125–7
Shellac, 72, 73, 96, 167
Shells, 36, 127
Silica gel, 134
Silicone paper, 169
Silicones, 161
Silk, 59, 60
Silver, 25, 49, 127–9
Silver plate, 125–7
Silverfish, 120
Slate, 130
Snuff bottles, 87
Soda crystals, 129, 133
Sodium bicarbonate, 38, 135, 158
Soft soap, 166
Solvents, 49, 94, 122, 170

Solvol Autosol, 16, 20, 42, 45, 50, 90,
    94, 96, 105, 107, 110, 122, 139,
    147, 148, 165
Soumaks, 39
Spelter (zinc), 35, 144, 145
Spit or Saliva, 12, 76
Splits, 40, 77, 98, 100, 119
Spode, 42
Stains, 12, 41, 42, 43, 63, 76, 88, 114,
    133, 137, 155
Stamps, 129, 130
Statues, 15, 35, 104, 105, 121, 130,
    133
Steaming, 118
Steel, 19, 37, 90, 91, 98, 165
Steradent, 43, 88, 133, 156
Stone, 36, 130, 158, 159
Stoneware, 42
Straw-work, 130
Stringing (on furniture), 64, 66, 67,
    78, 82
Suede cleaner, 100
Superglues, 43, 52, 53, 89, 94, 96,
    122, 151, 152
Surgical spirit, 170
Sylmasta, 16, 43, 52, 105, 156, 159
Synperonic N, 13, 15, 97, 115, 166,
    167

Talc, 35, 43
Tapestries, 143
Tarnish, 34, 128, 129
Taxidermy, 131, 132, 158
Tea caddies, 21, 121, 132, 133
Teapots, 34, 43, 133, 156
Tempera, 157
Terracotta, 42, 133
Textiles, 133–7, 158
Textiles, washing of, 136, 167
Thermo Lignum, 31, 117, 162
Thixofix, 37
Tiles, 42, 133
Tin, 34, 35, 138, 139
Titanium oxide, 105, 152, 159
Titanium white, 43, 93, 157
Tole, 138
Tools, 139
Topp's Ringaway, 76
Topp's Scratch Cover, 37
Torricelli, Evangelista, 23
Tortoiseshell, 16, 32, 33, 59, 60, 61,
    95, 121, 139, 140
Treen, 140

Turnery, 140
Tunbridge ware, 140, 141, 171
Turpentine, 18, 112, 157, 161, 167,
    168

UHU 16, 18, 29, 59, 89, 90, 93, 94,
    97, 105, 108, 113, 117, 127, 132,
    150
Ultraviolet light, 151, 154, 164
Upholstery, 141–3

Vacuum-cleaning, 26, 28, 30, 37, 40,
    41, 99, 104, 122, 141
Varnish, 21, 57, 59, 72, 85, 91, 96,
    111, 112, 118, 124, 132, 141, 168,
    171
Vaseline, 33, 88
Vellum, 117, 118
Velvet, 13, 113, 126, 127, 135
Veneers and veneering, 32, 61, 62, 70,
    78–82
Verdigris, 127, 129
Victoria & Albert Museum, 72
Vinegar, 88, 98, 127, 154, 161
Vulpex, 27, 99, 104, 113, 130, 164,
    166

Wallpaper adhesive, 101, 124
Warping, 83
Watches, 143, 144
Watercolour, 52, 85, 112, 114, 157
Water softener, 88
Wax, 41, 50, 67, 85, 93, 144
Wax fillers, 33, 73, 77, 94, 132, 159
Wax polish, 23, 27, 34, 49, 86, 92,
    129
Waxed paper, 32, 65, 169
Weapons, 18–21, 90, 167
Wedgwood, 36
White spirit, 14, 15, 21, 27, 30, 31,
    34, 36, 37, 41, 42, 93, 94, 99, 103,
    104, 105, 108, 112, 140, 169, 170,
    171
Whiting, 83, 149
Wood staining, 71, 77, 78, 171, 172
Woodworm, 26, 38, 57, 63, 99, 107,
    111, 117, 163
Wool, 13, 39, 40, 126, 127
Woolite, 56, 136, 167

Zebrite (graphite or black lead), 90,
    91, 157
Zinc (spelter), 35, 144, 145